GOOD EN

One Man's Memoir
on the Price of the Dream

BY DR. LEON BASS

Open Door Publications, LLC

Good Enough
One Man's Memoir on the Price of the Dream

Copyright © 2011 by Dr. Leon Bass

All rights reserved.
Printed in the United States

No part of this book may be used or reproduced in any manner whatsoever without the written permission of the author except in the case of brief quotations embodied in critical articles and reviews.

Published by
Open Door Publications
27 Carla Way
Lawrenceville, NJ 08648
www.OpenDoorPublications.com

Cover Design by
Vanessa Kitzie

ISBN: 9780982891841

★ TABLE OF CONTENTS ★

GOOD ENOUGH

★ FOREWORD ★

Imagine being a 14-year-old boy, arriving in Germany in the fall of 1944, fleeing the advancing Russian Army and arriving in a concentration camp called Buchenwald. I was absolutely sure that here, my life would come to an end. The idea of escape was on my mind. But how? And yet I could taste and feel the prospect of being free. And then days later, windows were splattered with stray bullets. Later still, I heard through the loud speaker that all SS were to leave immediately. And then everything fell silent! Very silent. Finally a voice came over the loud speaker — "Comrades, wir sind frei." We are free.

That was April 11, 1945. As I pulled myself up from the floor, I looked up towards the main entrance and saw the clock on top of the tower of Buchenwald. The time read 3:45 p.m. Then we saw American soldiers. We were euphoric. I will never forget the feeling! And then I saw soldiers that were completely different — they were black. I had never before seen a black person. I ran towards them. One held a camera taking photos. The other one had an overwhelming expression of compassion and love, and I noticed that he was moved by all that he saw. I attempted to touch and speak to them without much success. I was to find out many years later the names of the photographer, Sergeant William A. Scott, and the other one, Leon Bass.

In 1981, I was fortunate to recognize Leon in a photo as a young soldier in a B'nai B'rith magazine. At last I could touch him. At last I could speak to him. Since then, Leon Bass and I have become very good friends. We are soul mates. Our friendship is very precious and extremely meaningful and rewarding. We have appeared together in Vancouver, British Columbia, Seattle, Washington, and many other places. We are planning to meet in Tulsa, Oklahoma to speak to young students and adults, to tell them about the dangers of hate and discrimination, racism against African Americans and anti-Semitism against Jews. We both feel very strongly about sharing our respective experiences in the hope that the events we witnessed will offer an opportunity to reflect on the moral responsibilities of individuals as well as societies and governments.

Our stories remain a powerful lesson against racism and hatred, and they also reaffirm our commitment to uphold human rights for all and to value diversity. How is it possible that I, as a Jewish child destined to die, not only survived but lived to see this day? How is it possible that I would participate in this miracle in providing an introduction to my friend's memoirs? What a privilege!

There is a Jewish prayer in the Sheheyanu:
"Blessed are thou, 0 Lord our God, King of the universe, for thou hast kept us in life, and hast sustained us and enabled us to reach this season"
Leon and I have somehow reached this season of our lives – a blessing indeed.

Robbie Waisman

★ ACKNOWLEDGEMENTS ★

My life experiences began during those formative years with my mother and father. Their loving, caring and sacrificing helped me obtain the survival skills I needed as I entered the wider world.

The all-black elementary school that I attended in Philadelphia was an extension of my home. It was there that I was constantly reminded by my teachers that I was good enough to do and be all I wanted to do and be. With their encouragement I was able to overcome many of the obstacles I had to face, so I thank them for their gift of love.

As a beginning elementary school teacher, I was fortunate to have an outstanding and highly intelligent principal. His wisdom and sound advice helped me be successful in my first year of teaching. I remember his wise counseling when he said to me, "Leon, stand up, speak up, sit down and be appreciated." James Young had an impact on my educational experiences that I shall never forget.

The clarion voice of Dr. Martin Luther King, Jr. came out of the deep South and gave me the courage to challenge the racism that I experienced while serving as a soldier in the United States Army. His example has helped me in my everyday struggles to love the unlovable.

It was in 1971 that I met Nina Kaleska who was a survivor of the infamous concentration camp in Germany called Auschwitz. She came to speak to students at the Benjamin Franklin High School, but they were not listening to her. I came forward and admonished them for their rudeness. Nina asked me, "Did you tell them about your experiences?" Later, we shared mutual experiences about concentration camps. It was then that she said to me, "Young man, you have something to say. You should be telling everyone about your going into the Buchenwald Concentration Camp." I thank Nina for being the catalyst that started my speaking since that day.

Putting my memoirs in writing was due to Mary, my wife, who said, "You should put your experiences on the printed page." This was in the early 1990s. Speaking for me was easier than writing. But I listened to some of my friends whose experience in writing gave me the encouragement to try. My good friend Jeffry Lowenstein who wrote a column for a Chicago newspaper and other articles for an organization in Boston, Massachusetts, called "Facing History and Ourselves." He would keep me focused on my goal by his constant mantra, "Leon, how is your book progressing?" I owe him so much for making me want to succeed. There were times when some people in an audience who, after hearing me speak, would say, "Are you writing a book?" For all who felt my experience should be in writing, I extend my gratitude.

But there is one person who helped to bring my memoirs to a conclusion. Gloria Brown did this with her editing and correcting my many mistakes. She was patient through long weeks and months until the manuscript had come to its fruition.

I thank my dad whose words of wisdom made it possible for me to share my life experiences with my children and my grandchildren. He said to me, *"Son, keep your hands on the plow, hold on."*

GOOD ENOUGH

★ PREFACE ★

Somewhere I read that we are the sum total of all our experiences. My journey through life is comprised of experiences, both good and bad, and having reached the twilight of my years, I have felt compelled to share with my children and grandchildren some of those experiences and how they have impacted my life. This conviction became more urgent as age made the window of opportunity grow smaller. I knew that putting my experiences in writing would be difficult, but I also knew that I had to try.

During the peak of my professional years, the philosophies of Dr. Martin Luther King and Malcolm X were permeating our society. Embracing and promulgating some of those philosophies, especially those of Dr. King, required my taking positions on difficult issues. Therefore, I asked myself the question, "Is the price too high to stand up for what is right?" It was a difficult question, but for me the answer was "No, the price is not too high!" And I decided that I would be an agent for nonviolent change.

GOOD ENOUGH

★ CHAPTER ONE ★
THE EARLY YEARS

My parents were born in South Carolina around the turn of the century — my dad, Henry Cleveland Bass, in 1891, 26 years after the signing of the *Emancipation Proclamation,* and my mother, Nancy Weston Bass, in 1895. One year after my mother's birth, in 1896, the Supreme Court of the United States rendered its decision in the *Plessey v. Ferguson* case, upholding a Louisiana law that mandated "separate but equal" accommodations for blacks and whites and thus determining that the law was constitutional. This decision provided the legal justification for further social separation of blacks and whites and thus created a great deal of pain for people of color. "Jim Crow" became a way of life in our country, damaging both the oppressed and the oppressors.

In this environment, my parents struggled for an education, for food, for clothing and for a vestige of human dignity. Despite their struggle, they never lost faith in this country's potential to be a good place to live and raise a family. My father was a soldier in the United States Army and fought in France during World War I. He was told that he was fighting "to make the world safe for democracy." This was quite a contradiction when considering that people of color in this country were suffering racism and discrimination.

When the war ended, my father returned to South Carolina. He found that nothing had changed for the better,

My mother and father,
Henry Cleveland Bass
and Nancy Weston Bass

and he had had enough. He knew that there was not much of a future for him and his family in the racist environment of South Carolina, so he took my mother and their one child, my sister, Willabelle, and migrated north to Philadelphia.

It was in Philadelphia where five more children were born, all boys: Henry, Claude, Leon, Harvey and Marcellus. Our parents were caring and loving, and they protected us as much as possible from the pain they'd had to endure in South Carolina. They taught by example the values of love, honesty, loyalty, perseverance, hard work and respect for all people. These values were taught not by words alone, but by the way they lived.

I remember my mother working from early in the morning until late at night. She would clean the house from top to bottom, using a scrub board to clean what seemed to be a mountain of the family's dirty clothing. After dinner, there were dishes to be washed and food to be put in an ice box. During the evening, she would sew and mend our torn clothing, and on Saturday, she would starch and iron our clothing, especially the large numbers of white shirts. To this day, I don't know how she found the strength to do all of this and more for six children and a husband. I do remember the song she sang while fulfilling these tasks, "There is Something Within."

"There is something within me that's holding the rein;
There is something within I cannot explain."

My dad was a Pullman porter on the Pennsylvania railroad, and therefore, he was away from home for long periods of time. On his return, he would begin to repair things about the house. I was always happy when he allowed me to hand him the tools he needed as he made the repairs. Sometimes he would take the four youngest boys for walks through the neighborhood to give my mother a chance to relax. One of my favorite memories is of my father moving through the house singing and reciting poetry. One that he often recited began:

"Lives of great men all remind us
We can make our life sublime,
And departing leave behind us
Footprints on the sands of time."[1]

When we had chores to complete, he would recite these words:
"If a task is once begun, never leave it 'til it's done. Be the labor great or small, do it well or not at all."

---

[1] "Psalm of Life" by Henry Wadsworth Longfellow

No matter how well-intentioned, parents cannot completely insulate and protect young people from the ugliness of their environment. There comes a time when children must leave the nest and go out into the world.

When I was 5 years old, I was taken to the Martha Washington School, which had an all-black student body, because, as previously stated, the "separate but equal" decision of the Supreme Court prevailed. The principal, the teachers and all of the staff were black as well. In spite of this institutional racism, I know, in retrospect, that the quality of the educational program in this school was superb. The teachers had high standards and high expectations for all their students. The skills of reading, writing and computation were emphasized daily. In addition to our cognitive learning, we were also exposed to the arts. Our teachers would invite their friends to the school to share their many talents and experiences.

On one such occasion, a very tall, stately and imposing woman was introduced at an assembly program, but I did not hear her name because I was not paying attention during her introduction. Her hair was a mixture of black and gray; she wore a long black dress, and she appeared quite plain to me. She used a cane as she walked to the lectern to deliver her remarks.

I was in the third grade and knew nothing about the poem she began to recite, which I discovered later was entitled "The Prodigal Son" written by the black poet, James Weldon Johnson. She raised her cane as she spoke and pointed it at me in the audience and said in a loud booming voice, "Young man, young man, your arms too short to box with God!" I slouched down in my seat in an effort to hide, for I felt that she was speaking directly to me. It was many years later that I came to know about this dynamic personality. Her name was Mary McCloud

Bethune. I realize now that on that day in my formative years, I was in the presence of greatness.

This woman was a pioneer for educational excellence and educational opportunity for people of color. Born of parents who had been slaves, she learned early in life that education was the best way out of poverty. She founded a school in Daytona Beach, Florida, which today is known as Bethune-Cookman University. She was also an early civil rights leader and was an advisor to President Franklin Delano Roosevelt and friend to his wife, Eleanor Roosevelt.

I looked at these teachers with a great deal of awe and admiration, for they had achieved an education in spite of the system. They were my heroes. They too felt the price was not too high to do what was right. Each day they made me know that I was good enough to be all that I wanted to be if only I would be willing to work for it. The school became my home away from home.

When I was 5 or 6 six years of age, my big brother, Henry, was my hero. He was older and bigger than my other siblings. He was an outstanding athlete who could run like the wind and could play all sports. He was respected by his peers because he excelled in so many ways, but school for him was a disaster. One day it all came to a head as my father and Henry had a heated discussion about his grades and his truancy.

"I don't like school, and I'm dropping out!" Henry shouted.

"You have two choices. You go to school or you get a job," Dad shouted back.

Henry left home, but he didn't get a job. He survived for a few weeks on the largesse of a friend who permitted him to enter his house at night through a back bedroom window. There he would eat and sleep while his friend's mother was at work.

Soon his friend's mother discovered what had happened, and that was that. One day, I saw Henry talking to Dad at the front door. They reached an agreement, and Henry returned to school, but he soon dropped out again. This time he found a job at a Horn and Hardart Restaurant where he made little money, but it was a job.

Henry found another way to help the family. He left the Horn and Hardart to join the Civilian Conservation Corps. The CCC was a public work relief program for unemployed young men between the ages of 18 and 25. They worked on the infrastructure of our country's buildings and roads as part of President Roosevelt's New Deal legislation.

Along with the physical labor at the CCC camp, athletic opportunities were available. Henry enrolled in the boxing program and excelled as an amateur boxer, leading him to compete as a finalist in a statewide championship program for amateur boxers. My mother was opposed to his participation in what she referred to as a "gladiator sport," but Henry convinced her that it was a contest for beginners and no harm would come to him. Many of Henry's friends and acquaintances from the neighborhood went to the arena in Philadelphia to cheer him on. Later that night when my mother came home from church, Henry was stretched out on the couch in the parlor. He had lost his bout by a TKO, a technical knockout. My mother was glad to hear him say he was through with boxing.

A few years later, Henry left the Civilian Conservation Corps to work in the payroll office of the Marine Corporation in Philadelphia, an agency that procured clothing and equipment to distribute to our country's United States Marine Corps.

Shortly thereafter, on December 7, 1941, the Japanese attacked Pearl Harbor, and Henry was drafted for military service in the United States Navy. Fortunately, on the ship to which he was assigned, Henry met a journalist who helped him to set new goals for his life. Through their many conversations, Henry began to realize the value of an education, which led to his enrollment in the Navy's general education program where he earned his high school diploma. Three and a half years later, Henry was honorably discharged from military service.

It was when Henry returned to his job in the payroll office that his proficiency in mathematics was recognized. With encouragement from a friend, he attended classes in accounting and finance, which led to a succession of advancements to supervisor of the payroll office to Budget Analyst to Budget Specialist. Later, his expertise led to travel across the country speaking and advising high ranking Marine Corps officers on the procurement of clothing and equipment.

Henry retired from his job in 1998 to freelance as a mediator. His talents in this area were essential to settling racial unrest in Willingboro High School in New Jersey and in other similar issues across the United States. His reputation as a successful mediator led to his appointment as a board member and finally as President of the Board of Stockton State College in Pomona, NJ.

As he grew older, Henry became just like our father in so many ways. He viewed education as second only to Godliness, and he encouraged his children to pursue their education. All finished high school; two finished college, and one became an elementary school principal. Henry was my mentor; he encouraged me to go to graduate school, even lending me enough money to finish graduate school at Temple University.

Henry was my hero when I was small as much as when I was older, even though he violated the rules. I saw him as James Bond; he could take care of himself. Henry was a street fighter.

One day, a gang came down to our neighborhood, and the leader wanted to fight my brother because he had heard what a good fighter he was. All the other young men were urging Henry to fight; they knew he could take this other fellow in a minute.

But of course, since everyone in the neighborhood knew what was happening, my father heard about it also. My father came down to the street where this was going on, and he just stood there with his arms folded on his chest. My father never said anything. I watched my dad. He never said a word. Henry watched him, too. He knew what our dad stood for. The fight never took place.

This was the middle of the Depression, and even my father was working only on a part-time basis, so soon we found ourselves receiving the dreaded welfare. To be on welfare was to be at the bottom. My parents viewed it as shameful, and they tried to keep it to themselves, but as I got older I could see the cans of food that came into the house, and I knew where they came from.

I didn't really talk about it with them, or with anyone else. It wasn't something you talked about with your friends, even though you knew that clothing might be passed around to someone in the neighborhood who needed it. My mother had a friend who worked in a wealthy woman's kitchen, and sometimes she had food left over from there to share. I remember walking several miles with my brothers to get the food and bring it back.

In the early 1930s I was hired as a paper boy, and my paper route covered a large area, so I got to know the community. With every passing day, I discovered how strong and resilient many of my neighbors were. I saw the situations many people were living under. We were poor, but many people were worse off.

As a paper boy I would go to many different homes and learn a lot of things about people in the community that I wouldn't have known otherwise. I will never forget one home where I delivered papers. There were a lot of young ladies living there, and they'd be coming and going up and down the stairs in their bathrobes. It was a brothel, of course. There would be men sitting around the table drinking, and they'd try to hide their face from me because they knew my dad or they were the father of a friend of mine. But I never said a word about who I saw there.

It was good for me to see so many different homes and different situations. Some people didn't let poverty dictate the values they lived by; others did. But overall I saw mostly positive things. It was a neighborhood, and people looked out for each other, and each other's children. These same neighbors would inform my parents if I failed to behave appropriately. They were an extended family, and their caring helped me to avoid getting into trouble.

One day I was walking down the street, and there was a truck full of apples. I took one of the apples, but the driver saw. He raised his arm and said he'd tell my father. I dropped the apple and ran. He didn't tell my father, and I never did either.

Sadness came to our home when my sister, Willabelle, left. I was about 10 years old, and she was only 17. Exactly why she left, I never knew, even to this day, but as I got older and thought about it, I knew she had not been happy. My mom believed that girls should be at home cooking and cleaning. While the boys were allowed to play football and go out with friends in the evening, my sister never had a birthday party, she never had a date. Once I saw her walking home from school with a young man. I knew he was popular in school, and he was walking close to her and carrying her books. But when they were a few blocks from home he gave her books back to her and went another way. He never came close to the house. She would never have been comfortable bringing him home for my mother to meet him.

My mother cried a lot when my sister left, but she finally found solace in religion after attending a revival meeting at a fundamentalist church. Prior to this time, my mother had not attended church. My dad would take the four youngest in the family to a Baptist church whenever he was home from his job.

Like most young and active boys, going to church was not to my liking. We had to wear our short pants and sat on

benches with mohair cushions that were very scratchy and uncomfortable. When my mother joined the fundamentalist church, she prevailed upon my father to attend with us, and in time the youngest of us four children attended regularly, too. The members of that church were caring and kind to all of us. As a teenager of about twelve, I became interested in learning about the religious philosophy the church promulgated.

My mother's mother; I don't know her name, she was just Grandma. She was from the Cree Indian tribe.

This curiosity led to my questioning their belief that salvation could only come to those who believe and accept Jesus Christ as their personal savior. Those failing to do so were, in their judgment, damned. That was the beginning of my search to find a religion that was supportive to me.

When I told my mother I couldn't go to this church anymore she didn't say too much, she just accepted my choice. My mother was always very stoic; she didn't show emotion. I sometimes thought this trait came from my grandmother, who was Cree.

Willabelle was gone for about 4 years. At first I didn't know where she was, but one day I learned that she was living just a few blocks away with my aunt and uncle. One summer evening when I came home, I saw my sister sitting in the parlor with my Uncle John, Dad's oldest brother. She was now 21 years of age. She looked so beautiful. My mother came home from church and walked into the parlor. I had never seen my mother as happy as she was on seeing Willabelle.

"I knew it would happen; I knew it would happen!" she said. She kept patting her breast as she held her Bible close to her. After that, the relationship between my mother and Willabelle changed. They were more than just mother and daughter, they were good friends.

Music had a salutary effect on life when my Uncle Harry, Aunt Amy's husband, and other Pullman porters would bring their musical instruments to our home. (Aunt Amy, my mother's sister, was married to Dad's brother, Uncle Harry. In other words, two sisters married two brothers.) These gatherings were more social than musical, but I was influenced by the efforts of this small group to make music. Uncle Harry played the trumpet and provided the leadership the group needed.

When my parents became aware of my interest in music, they felt that piano lessons would develop that interest. For several years, I gave cursory attention to my piano lessons, but it became obvious to my parents that my other interests, namely baseball, football and other sports, were competing with the piano lessons; therefore music was the loser.

The parlor in our home was considered off limits to all of my siblings, but the piano lessons made it accessible to me at any time. During those practice sessions, I discovered a group of bound books close to where I sat. This was the beginning of my exposure to some of the classics. Victor Hugo's *Les Miserables* and *The Hunchback of Notre Dame* were two of my favorites.

In addition to being a musician, Uncle Harry was a man of many talents. He had been a student at Hampton University where he majored in engineering. His love of science motivated him to become an inventor while working as a Pullman porter. It was in my adult years that I found out that Uncle Harry had invented and patented a timer. His contribution to the world was a switch that would turn on the lights in your home when you were absent. Many other appliances could then be made operative using a timer. There were businessmen who sought to buy his patent, but they did not offer Uncle Harry the financial remuneration he expected. These industrialists waited until the expiration of the 20-year paten,t which then gave anyone the right to manufacture his invention without his authorization. Uncle Harry and his wife never received any compensation for his invention, but by turning down the industrialists' offers, Uncle Harry knew he had done the right thing, and the price for his dignity was not too high.

In 1933, I was promoted to the seventh grade in the integrated Sulzberger Junior High School. The school's pupil population was approximately 70% white and 30% black with a 100% white teaching staff, but when I reached the ninth grade, a black art teacher was assigned to the school. I remember how proud all of the black students were to see our race represented on the faculty, but it would be many years before real desegregation of the staff took place at the high schools.

While at Sulzberger, I experienced no overt acts of racism, and for the first time in my young life, I had a friend who was white. Leonard Blumberg and I were both in the academic section and sat next to each other in many of our classes. One day, I had nothing to eat for lunch. I didn't tell Leonard, but he knew and gave me 3 cents of the 10 cents he had. We never spoke of his random act of kindness. Our friendship lasted for 3 years but never extended beyond the school day. I never visited his home nor he mine. Without being told, we both knew that racism had put limits on our relationship. After completing the ninth grade, Leonard was assigned to Overbrook High School; I was assigned to West Philadelphia High School, and sadly, we were never to meet again.

My high school academic achievement was average. This was due to poor study habits and a lack of motivation, although my grades in English were good because of my love for literature. History and Physical Education helped to boost my grade level too, but the rest of my grades were average.

In January of 1943, I graduated from West Philadelphia High School and secured a job working at the Reading Mail Terminal in downtown Philadelphia. This was arduous, back-breaking work loading bulk mail on the box cars. This laborious work experience convinced me that I needed an education beyond high school.

GOOD ENOUGH

★CHAPTER TWO★
ARMY BASIC TRAINING

In my attempt to avoid hard labor, I decided to join the Army. It was 1943; I was 18 years old and just out of high school, and it was there that I came face to face with institutionalized racism. On the day of my induction into the United States Army, I went down to the induction center in Philadelphia with some other boys who had just graduated high school with me; all white. The day high school ended we walked down from the school to center city. I was totally unaware of what I was about to encounter. We were excited. At the induction center the great awakening came. My parents had insulated us as much as possible from racism as we were growing up. Of course, I knew it existed, but it wasn't on my mind that day. I was going to do what my father had done: join the Army and serve my country.

When we reached the door of the armory, a sergeant was standing there. He took one look at me and said, "Go this way," pointing to the right. He looked at my white friends and said, "Go this way," pointing to the left. We were separated because in 1943 all of the armed forces were segregated. My country practiced and promulgated institutional racism. By doing so, my country was saying to me, "Leon, you are not good enough to serve with white soldiers because you are black." This was the beginning of many racist policies and practices I experienced and endured on my tour of duty in the United States Army.

I would be part of a totally black unit with about 600 other young men from the area. We were given a time to catch the train, and I went home to tell my parents what I'd just done. My dad was concerned when I told him, but he tried not to show it.

My mom was not happy, but as always, she kept her feelings inside. She just proceeded to go down to the basement and iron clothes. That's what she did when she was upset. I saw that her nose was red when she came back up. There was nothing I could do, of course. I was already signed up, so I just said, "Goodbye, I'll get in touch," and left. I wanted to get away from the pressure that was building up inside me.

A few days later I was in Ft. Meade, Maryland. We got our injections and a lot of aptitude tests, and then were sent south to Columbus, Georgia. It was an interesting trip south. My mother had been born in a small town outside of Columbia, South Carolina, but I'd never been there. My father would go back sometimes to visit his brother, and I'd asked to go with him, but my mother wouldn't let me. She was worried I wouldn't know how to act in the South. She told me, "You don't know enough not to get yourself killed."

Well, Uncle Sam took me down to South Carolina. I saw the sign for Columbia and I knew I'd just arrived in the place my mother thought I should never go. We passed on by South Carolina and headed into Georgia. When we arrived the officers assembled all of us and right away began to teach us the rules and regulations. We learned to turn right, turn left, about face. We walked away from there and went to Camp Wheeler for infantry basic training. This was where I was going to learn how to be a soldier. I learned how to salute, and who to salute, and when, and all the things I was supposed to do to show respect to the officers; and all of the officers were white. I was learning just exactly how racism was going to affect my life.

Our battalion had to go through 3 months of infantry basic training, and the skills that I had to master were so rigorous and arduous that I thought the regimen was designed to prevent me from succeeding. But with time, I discovered that their methods did promote discipline and perseverance as well as proficiency.

The close order drills and the 25-mile hikes, while grueling, I endured and accomplished successfully. But one area that I found particularly difficult was the sending and receiving of Morse Code. We were broken up into sections based on the testing we had had. I was put into the headquarters company because I had finished high school, but when it got to learning Morse Code, I had trouble. Some of the men picked it up right away, but I just couldn't tune into it. I struggled with it, and eventually they put me in the Intelligence Reconnaissance section.

Our job was to go out and see things, to learn how to use surveying instruments, to judge the weight of bridges and things like that. I had a lot easier time with these skills than I'd had with Morse Code. The rigorous part, which we all had to do, was to hike for 25 miles with a full pack on our backs. First we hiked 10 miles, then 15, then 25. When we reached that milestone we knew we had now reached the point of being good soldiers. We also had to learn to take care of our packs, our shoes and all of our belongings. We had to learn the manual of arms and how to use a rifle. (Never call it a gun!) We had to learn how to take it apart and put it back together so well we could do it blindfolded.

We were learning how to survive under fire while guns were going off over our heads.

There was a difference between what we did in the field with the white officers and what we did in the barracks. We learned a lot about each other; one fellow told me I'd never make it to be a sergeant because I didn't know how to cuss.

We had a lot of fun in the barracks. One fellow played the saxophone; another played drums. We would dance and tell stories. It was both interesting and fun a lot of the time.

Of course, I also learned to keep tabs on my belongings. One day I wanted to go to town, but when I went to put on my clothes I found another fellow had taken them and had already left. I couldn't go that day because I didn't have the right clothes to wear. Later he put them back; I didn't cuss or call names. I just told him how it had made me feel, and I think he respected that I didn't start a fight. You're in trouble when you start fighting.

I also remember another day when I was coming out of the shower with just a towel around my waist and flip flops on my feet. We'd had our hair cut, and they'd about shaved me bald; when the other fellows saw me in the towel and flip flops with a shaved head they called me Mahatma Gandhi.

One day I met some fellows from Coatesville, Pennsylvania, who knew my brother, Harvey. Harvey had spent several years in Coatesville at a reform school there because he was always getting into trouble. They told me my brother really knew how to fight. That was when I first began to learn what life had been like for Harvey growing up, and I felt so sorry for him. The school was one of those places where you constantly had to fight just to survive.

Meeting those men was when I first began to get insight into my younger brother.

Harvey was always independent and marched to a different drum. He was shooting pool at the pool hall with grown men when he was only about 12 years old. Harvey was looking for something different in life than I was, it seemed. I've never really understood how two people can grow up with the same parents, in the same home, and come out so different. He loved to drink and smoke and fight. He was the opposite of me and of our parents.

We had two cousins from South Carolina who came to live with us for awhile, Willy Ray and Robbie Weston. Willy Ray and Harvey never got along well, maybe because they were both very competitive, and if Harvey thought someone had done something to him he'd bide his time and wait to get even. One day Harvey saw Willy Ray shooting marbles, so he hid behind a hedge, and when he got the chance he hit Willy Ray in the head with a rock, then he took off running. That was Harvey.

Even later in life he lived in his own world and was disconnected from the rest of the family. Once in a while I would see him at a wedding or a funeral; he never stayed long, he'd go off with some of the other cousins who were into drinking. He got married and had a couple of children. He drank a lot and eventually became an alcoholic, and his wife left him. Harvey never had a good paying job. He worked for a while for a security firm, and then as a bartender.

But that was to be in the future. In World War II, Harvey ended up in the Navy, and while I was in basic training I came across him in Memphis, Tennessee. I'd had leave and had gone to Memphis for a visit and ran into Harvey. It was good to see him, and we got a chance to visit together several times. In the Navy he was a machinist's mate. He would go up with the pilots while they were testing the planes. Once he was in a plane crash and survived; but I've always wondered if that didn't make him worse.

Throughout the demanding training period, racism was ever present. I remember the day when our entire battalion was assembled, and a white woman was escorted through our ranks. She was looking for a black soldier who was alleged to have raped her. Fortunately, no one in our company was identified as the culprit. I never heard anything more about her or the incident; I never knew if she identified someone in another unit. All I knew at the time is that if she accused someone he was going to go to jail. It didn't seem right that she could just walk among us and pick someone out. We all knew that white people said all blacks looked alike.

So many different little incidents took place during that time, and we talked a lot about racism in the barracks when no white officers were around. I was trying to be the best soldier I could be, but it still bothered me that my country kept telling me in so many ways that I wasn't good enough.

There were also group motivation sessions for all of the black soldiers. The Army knew that many of us felt we were fighting for something we weren't allowed to enjoy ourselves. The motivation sessions had a title, "Why We Fight." Of course, we discussed the exact same topic when we were by ourselves and no officers could hear us. We felt more secure in sharing what we thought when we were by ourselves.

Once, during a motivation session, our white platoon leader, a first lieutenant from Georgia, called on me to give my understanding of why we were fighting this war. For the first time in my young life I felt I had something to say.

"We fight to preserve and protect our fundamental rights and privileges as American citizens, but for those of us who are call 'colored,' these rights and privileges have been denied. Therefore, we must fight the enemy abroad and the enemy at home if liberty and justice for all is to have any real meaning," I said.

The group's silence after hearing my remarks was deafening. The white officer told the group of soldiers to take a break, and then he called me aside.

"In my town the colored people don't do anything to deserve to be treated like the white folk. They don't go to school. They are always getting into fights. They don't work…"

I was listening, and I began to get very angry.

"Private Bass, when you're in Rome you do as Romans do," the officer continued.

"Sir, I am an American, and we are in America, so I want to do as Americans do," I replied.

The Georgian officer's face turned red at my remarks, but he was silent, and from that day on, he treated me with respect. That was the first time I ever expressed my feelings on race, and I learned there were consequences. The soldiers who heard my remarks questioned the wisdom of speaking out against racism in the military. They were concerned that my assertiveness would bring down the wrath of that white lieutenant as well as others. I was isolated by the way I felt. I stopped talking to others about my feelings or experiences.

The experiences I had in the military hurt, but there was so little I could do about it. I had to keep it inside. I tried hard to live up to my parents' belief that you had to love the unlovable. I was 18 years old and had to go through 3 years of keeping it to myself and becoming a very angry soldier. I came to the realization that the damage wasn't just to me. The people who were treating me in this way were also being hurt. The officer who told me, "When in Rome do as the Romans do," was trying to justify the treatment our country accorded its "colored" citizens by blaming the victims for their condition.

It was near the end of our basic training when I was summoned to the battalion commander's office. He informed me that my Uncle Jack, Mom's brother, had died and that I was eligible for an emergency furlough. If I accepted his offer, I would miss the last week of our training out in the field. I asked if missing this last week of training would mean I would have to repeat the entire training program with another unit. The answer was "Yes." As much as I wanted to pay my respects to Uncle Jack, needless to say, I turned down the offer of that emergency furlough.

★ ★ ★

While at Camp Wheeler, our entire battalion was assembled one day, and we were marched to a theater to see a film that featured a black singer named Lena Horne. This was to be the first appearance of this beautiful black actress in a major film. We watched the entire film only to discover that in the version of the film shown on our base her role as a singer had been deleted because of her skin color.

This racist act caused vocal outrage by the black soldiers. To rectify this blatant act of racism, the film was shown again the next day with the Lena Horne segment included. This abated the anger and enhanced the morale of the soldiers in our battalion.

In late August 1943, the battalion received orders to go to Camp McCain in Mississippi. This change in our location was ordered because our unit was designated as combat engineers. We had now become the 183rd Engineer Combat Battalion. For me, moving from Georgia to Mississippi was like going from the frying pan into the fire. This camp, I soon learned, had the worst facilities one could imagine. We were stationed there for approximately a year, and in that time I experienced some of the most blatant racism that I had ever seen.

I wanted to visit Tougaloo College, a historically black college located seven miles north of Jackson, Mississippi. To purchase a bus ticket, I had to go to the nearby town of Granada. When I got to the bus stationed I noticed how pretty and clean it was. I'd been in Georgia long enough that when I saw a building like that I knew enough to think, "Will I be allowed into this building?" I looked around and saw that the other black people were going around to the back, so I walked up an alley filled with trash, the smell of urine and ladies of the evening plying their trade. Once inside I had to stand in a separate line with a few other black customers and wait until the ticket agent finished serving all the white customers and finally came to the window to sell me a ticket. A white man came up behind me and said, "Mary, you got any niggers that need to be cut?" He pretended he was joking but it was a threat, and he was the bus driver.

Philadelphia had had its share of racism; I knew that, but it didn't affect me personally there the way it did in the South. If I wanted to go to the movies there was a black theater or I could sit in the balcony at the white theater. There were stores I could go to if I wanted to buy something. My parents had tried to keep us away from the ugliness as much as possible. They talked about the way it was when they were growing up in South Carolina, but this was the first time I'd experienced it personally. I experienced many incidents of racism in Mississippi, but none was as frightening as that day.

As I boarded the bus, I looked up and read the sign on the bus. It read, "Colored must sit at the rear of the bus." I went to the back of the bus, but I found that all of the seats for people of color were occupied, so I had to stand. There were other times, and I kid you not, when I had to stand on a bus for more than 100 miles looking at empty seats that I could not occupy. It is strange to see empty seats and know you can't sit down.

I questioned my wisdom in joining the army as I looked at that sign that was saying to me that I was not good enough. I took a seat in the white section.

"Boy!" The bus driver saw me and called out as I sat down.

I did not answer, so he called again, "Boy!"

I looked out the window, ignoring him. It was then that a little old black woman came over to me and said, "He's calling you, son."

"No ma'am, he's calling a boy; I'm a man," I said.

The bus driver, with hate in his eyes, came back to where I was sitting and said, "Do you see that sign?"

"I can't read." I answered.

"Well we'll damn right show you!" he replied angrily and turned and hurried to the front of the bus.

"Lordy, son, you better move or they are going to kill you!" the old black woman said to me.

I had heard that bus drivers carried guns in their glove compartment and I realized that this was one of those times when "discretion was the better part of valor," so I moved to the back of the bus, but I was so angry I can't begin to describe how I felt. Saying that I couldn't read was an expression of my anger; it was playing their game. My parents had advised me early on in life that there were limits to what I could do and what I could say; they had tried to insulate me from the ugliness.

But still, I carried this anger at the system for those limits. This was the first time I had ever stood up to an authority figure telling me I couldn't do something. He wanted to let me know that I wasn't strong enough by myself to stand up to the system.

Again, I was being told that I was not good enough. Those people had already decided that I was not good enough to sit in any empty seat reserved for whites on that bus. The racist and denigrating behavior by the bus driver and the white passengers impacted my life. I was dressed in the uniform of an American soldier. I had taken an oath to defend these people with my life if that became necessary. What a damnable experience to have when you are 18 years of age and you have volunteered to serve your country.

I was so infuriated by this experience that I failed to thank that little old black woman for her kindness. She was my guardian angel and probably saved my life on that bus in Mississippi, but when the bus stopped she disappeared so quickly I never saw her leave.

In spite of this racism, I would often go to Tougaloo College to visit the young ladies who I had met at a dance in Camp McCain. When I entered the gates of Tougaloo College, I felt as if I had left the state of Mississippi and all the evil that existed there.

Many years later I was watching a program on PBS about the Jews who left Germany shortly before the start of the war, particularly because of the Kristallnacht incident. Kristallnacht, the "Night of Broken Glass," was a series of attacks against the Jews throughout Germany and Austria. It took place November 9 and 10, 1938. Jewish homes, shops and towns were ransacked by both German SA storm troopers and civilians. During the incident about 1,668 synagogues were ransacked and 30,000 Jewish men – a quarter of all Jewish men in Germany — were taken to concentration camps where they were tortured for months.

When I watched the program I learned that many of the Jews who left Germany and came to the United States at that time were very well educated people, often teachers. They had difficulty finding jobs at the white colleges but several of the historically black schools such as Howard and Tougaloo College took them in and gave them teaching jobs. When I was visiting there I never knew that. Out of the ugliness of racism something worthwhile had come.

Both the Jews and the blacks had a common problem with racism, and they banded together to help each other.

My weekends at Tougaloo were wonderful but all too brief. The final phase of our training as combat engineers took us into Texas and Louisiana to engage in war games. It was in this setting that we encountered other black soldiers assigned to combat units. They told us to avoid some of the small black communities where white soldiers would go. They said that the white soldiers were visiting the black prostitutes there, and they wanted to keep the black soldiers from doing the same.

Our last day of training in Mississippi was spent in a large wooded area outside of a small town call Duck Hill. There were stories of how three little black boys, while playing under a small bridge, allegedly had looked up the dresses of young white girls. Several white men, after hearing this story, went out to a bridge and hanged all three of these young boys.

Our training exercise required us to shoot blanks at airplanes that were attacking our encampment. When we completed the exercise, all blank cartridges were to be turned in to the supply sergeant. Some of the soldiers decided to keep their blank ammunition. They knew that they would be returning to base through that little town of Duck Hill where those boys had been hanged.

I didn't know anything about what they planned to do. As we came through that town I was assigned to direct traffic at a crossroad. The trucks came speeding into the town, and as they approached the intersection, some of the soldiers began firing their rifles using the blank cartridges. The townspeople began to run for cover into their houses and stores. When the last truck had passed, some of the townspeople came back outside. I was left as the lone soldier standing on the roadside waiting to be picked up by the last jeep in the convoy. It was a harrowing few minutes for me. As the trucks drove away and the sound of gunfire ceased, the townspeople began to come back out on the street, and there I was. I had no ammunition; it was verboten to give us real ammunition, but I slammed my rifle shut with a loud click to make them think that my rifle was loaded. All I could think was that if these people would hang little children, what would they do to me? Finally the jeep came and picked me up. The next day the camp commander came to the camp with some of the town officials seeking an explanation for what had taken place in the town. Fortunately, no one person was singled out for punishment.

***

After completing our war games, we received orders to leave Camp McCain and report to Camp Joseph T. Robinson on the outskirts of Little Rock, Arkansas. It was at this location that we prepared for overseas duty.

GOOD ENOUGH

★ CHAPTER THREE ★
OVERSEAS DUTY

Late in September of 1944, we arrived in Taunton, Massachusetts. One week later, our unit, the 183rd Engineer Combat Battalion, sailed for England. Our troop ship landed at Liverpool, and from there we traveled by train to a small community called Fordingbridge, Hants. This would prove to be a welcome relief for me after the racism I had encountered in the United States. The people in this community received us with open arms. We had been in the community of Fordingbridge for only a few days when the community held a dance to welcome us to England. It was my good fortune to meet Diane Coleman, an attractive young woman. She had come to the dance with her family, who were the proprietors of a bakery and a butcher shop. Diane and I danced quite often during that evening. When the dance was over I thanked her for a lovely evening and said good night to her parents.

The following day was Sunday, and I was relaxing with some of my friends where we were billeted. We were all members of the battalion's intelligence reconnaissance section. I did not know that Captain Ellis, who was in charge of our section, had met Diane Coleman before I had. It became quite apparent that I had usurped his station with Diane at the dance. Nevertheless, he came to our billet that Sunday morning to tell me that I was invited to the Coleman's home for dinner for being so nice to their daughter. This white officer, from the state of Virginia, had to tell me, a black soldier, that I was to have dinner with a young white female. His face was red, but he delivered the invitation. This invitation for dinner became a weekly event, and I looked forward to being with my newfound friends.

Diane would spend the week in London where she attended secretarial school, but on the weekends she came home to be with her family. On weekends it was customary for some members of the community to visit the local pub to socialize. Diane and I would sometimes go there to play darts while her family sat and drank bitters.

On one occasion, I went to London to meet Diane. We had made plans to go to the Haymarket Theatre to see John Gielgud playing in Shakespeare's *Hamlet*. After this excellent and exciting experience, we enjoyed dinner at a nearby restaurant. I accompanied Diane to the train taking her back home, and I took my train to return to Fordingbridge. Little did I know, I would never see her again. Our unit immediately received orders to go to France, and although Diane and I corresponded for a while, we soon lost touch.

Early in December, our battalion left England from Southampton. We crossed the English Channel to La Havre, France. We parked on the side of a road outside of a small town where we were to wait for orders — orders that would tell us what our battalion's responsibility would be in fighting this war. It was now 1944 and close to the Christmas season. The weather was severe, snow was everywhere and the temperature was well below zero.

We were there only about a week before receiving our orders. The battalion had been attached to the Third Army under the leadership of General George Patton, and our mission was to go into Belgium to a small town called Martelange.

Upon our arrival in the town the captain and I, along with several other soldiers, were sent to reconnoiter the outskirts of the town. I was driving the vehicle, and all of the other soldiers were in the back of the truck, which had its canvas sides rolled down to keep out the cold. The only two people who could be seen in the truck were me and the captain, who was white.

We were quite a distance from the area when three figures, dressed all in white and armed with rifles, rose out of a snow bank. We were ordered to halt and to give the password, which we had not been given that day. Our captain was ordered to step out of the vehicle. One of the soldiers looked in the driver's side of our truck and saw me. He said, "Everything is okay; they are Americans." The captain said nothing, but I believe that this white southerner felt he was lucky, on this night, to be part of a battalion of black soldiers.

In the town of Martelange, there was a bridge that had been completely destroyed by the enemy, and our mission was to rebuild that bridge. We had to do this because up the highway about 15 kilometers, there was another small town called Bastogne in which there were American soldiers, some of whom were members of the 101st Airborne Division, who had been trapped in that town. Their lives were in jeopardy, and they had to be rescued. General Patton and other members of the allied forces began to prepare for a rescue mission.

GOOD ENOUGH

The Siege of Bastogne was one small portion of the Battle of Bulge, one of the most important and deadly battles of World War II. The Germans attempted to break through the Allied lines and reach the harbor at Antwerp, Belgium, seizing roadways throughout eastern Belgium. Because all seven main roads in the Ardennes mountain range converged on the town of Bastogne, its control was vital to the German attack. The siege of Bastogne lasted from December 20 to December 27.

In order to get up to Bastogne, many of the soldiers would have to cross the bridge that we were going to build in Martelange. We worked on the bridge night and day. In spite of the weather we worked; in spite of shelling by the enemy's 88 howitzers we worked; in spite of the airplanes that came every night strafing machine gun bullets while trying to bomb the bridge we worked; in spite of the land mines that were everywhere, we worked on the bridge. We finished that bridge on time, in 5 days, and all the men, tanks, guns and ammunition crossed it. They went up to Bastogne and helped to rescue those men.

I lost a cousin in the Battle of the Bulge. He was in a red ball transportation unit. I knew he was stationed near where we were building our bridge. One day a friend of his came to me to tell me he had been killed. It was William Ray Weston, my mother's brother's son who had come to Philadelphia and lived with us for awhile before the war. Willy Ray's truck ran over a land mine while he was carrying a load of ammunition. They never found the body.

When I heard about his death I wrote a letter home to my mother and father telling them how sorry I was that I had joined the army. Willy Ray had died fighting for freedom and democracy for others when, at home, he didn't have those things himself. A black warrant officer came to me with the letter a few days after I had mailed it. Everything we mailed was read by the censors then, and they would cut out, with scissors, anything they thought

45

could give information to the enemy or could be demoralizing at home. Because of the censors, the officers told me, my letter just couldn't be sent. I watched him as he tore it up.

Building that bridge was a wonderful experience for the men in the 183rd Engineer Combat Battalion. It was a glorious day in my life. This experience of our unit's participation in the Battle of the Bulge strengthened and confirmed our belief that we were good enough. But I soon found out that whenever you fight a war you pay a heavy price for glory. I realized this one day while standing alongside the road in the snow.

Several trucks were passing by. They were grave-registration trucks filled with the bodies of American soldiers piled high atop one another. As I looked at that scene, I said to myself, "Leon, why did you join the army? What are you doing in this place? You could end up that way." I pondered the many indignities I had experienced during the days of my basic training. I remembered the question I was asked by the platoon leader in Georgia, "Leon, what are you fighting for?"

That question became very real to me as I witnessed death and dying in Belgium. I remembered that I, a black soldier, could not get a drink of water at a public water fountain back home. I could not get a meal in a restaurant back home, and they would not let me have a seat on a bus back home. So what was I doing here? What was I fighting for? I didn't have all the answers to my questions. I was only 19 years old at the time. But I was an angry young black soldier. I was angry at my country because my country was using and abusing me. I was angry because my country was placing me in harm's way to fight and perhaps to die to preserve all those rights and privileges every American should enjoy, but at the same time, my country was letting me know, in so many different ways, that it thought I was not good enough to enjoy what I was fighting for.

Plans for our battalion to leave the area were being made, but the reconnaissance section had to reconnoiter the area first. That day we discovered another bridge that had been destroyed by the enemy. I drove close to the bridge and knew there was no chance for our battalion to get across. I turned my vehicle around and backed it on each shoulder of the road. The next day I went back to see if any effort was being made to rebuild the bridge. Nothing had been done in that regard, but to my amazement, there were two trucks that had been blown apart by land mines placed on both sides of that road.

As I pondered the situation, I realized that my truck had made the same turns in that same area but without any mishap. I believe I was spared because the temperature was far below the freezing point when I was there the day before, and the temperature kept those land mines from exploding. However, on the day following my trip, there was a thaw, which allowed the mines to detonate and blow up those other two vehicles. I believe some higher force looked down on me with tender loving care and said, "It is not your time to die. I have work for you to do."

As we were driving our vehicles away from the town of Wiltz, toward Germany, we passed infantry soldiers walking in a long line on each side of the road. As I drove past them, one of the soldiers looked at me and yelled, "Fellas, look! We are winning the war because the niggers are here." This denigrating remark confirmed to me that the racism I was encountering in Europe was home-grown in America.

GOOD ENOUGH

This photo shows me and a few other members of the
183rd at Buchenwald. I am the second solider on the left.
The picture was taken by William A. Scott III, a sergeant in
my company. His family owned a newspaper in Georgia,
the *Atlanta Daily World*, and he had brought his camera
with him overseas.

★ CHAPTER FOUR ★
A JOURNEY INTO HELL

In the spring of 1945 our battalion was ordered to go up into East Germany. We drove through the rest of France, Belgium, Germany and over the Rhine River. We saw Frankfurt, Cologne, Dusseldorf, Osenak and finally Nurenberg — places that I had only read about. We were winning the war.

We were living on a farm, and as a city boy I found almost everything I saw there amazing. But while the farm animals and farm life may have seemed almost normal, the war intruded on a regular basis.

The winter had been hard, and snow was piled high everywhere. As it began to thaw, discoveries were made. One day I saw a hand sticking out of a snow pile near our camp. When they pulled up the body they found it was an American soldier. I never heard how he had died. On another night I was walking over to where some of the fellows were gambling; it was icy out and hard to see. I slipped on the ice, and when I put my hands out to break my fall, they landed on a body. The face was almost down to the bone. I did learn more about how this man had died. He was an American pilot whose plane had gone down. After building the bridge and the recognition we had received I had just begun to feel more positive about what I was doing as a black man in this war. After those two incidents my good feelings were lost.

We drove our vehicles a short distance from Weimar and set up our camp. A lieutenant in the battalion's Intelligence Reconnaissance section, of which I was a part, came over to me and two others and told us to take our gear and rifles and come with him. We followed him and boarded a truck.

I asked, "Where are we going?"

"We're going to a concentration camp," he responded.

It was April 12, 1945, one day after the concentration camp at Buchenwald was liberated by American soldiers.

Thinking back on it now, I'm not really sure why he wanted us with him that day. Maybe he didn't feel safe. I don't know. It was the army, and you went where you were told. I didn't know anything about concentration camps. In all my training, no one ever mentioned concentration camps. On this day, I was to have the shock of my life. I was going to walk into a concentration camp called Buchenwald.

Buchenwald was established by the Nazis in June of 1937. It was one of the first and largest of the concentration camps. Between April of 1938 and April of 1945, approximately 238,380 people of many nationalities and religious backgrounds, including 350 Western Allied POWs, were incarcerated there. The exact number of deaths that took place is not known, but one estimate is 56,000 in that 7-year period. Buchenwald was not considered an "extermination camp" by the Nazis, but rather a labor camp. Cause of death included starvation and human experimentation. Other prisoners were simply shot or hanged.

When I entered the camp that day I knew nothing of this. I only knew what I saw in front of me. I now call them the walking dead. I saw human beings who had been tortured, beaten, starved and denied everything that would make life worth living. The things I saw were so horrible that while I was there I didn't really react to it. I was just shocked. I was 20 years old, and nothing in my life had prepared me for this.

There they stood, many with sores on their bodies due to malnutrition, some dressed in pajamas, others naked. One man held up his hands. His fingers had been webbed together with scabs due to the malnutrition. These people were just skin and bone. They had skeletal faces with deep-set eyes, and their heads had been clean-shaved. I had never seen anything like this in all of my experiences — nothing like this. They had been denied everything.

They began to move, stumbling toward me, holding onto one another just to keep from falling, and as they did so, they began to speak. They were speaking in many different languages, and I could not understand any of it, so I backed away. I said to myself, "Who are these people? What have they done that was so terrible that anyone would treat them this way?" I didn't know the answer.

There was a young Polish man there escorting us who understood and spoke the English language well. He began to tell us about Buchenwald. He said, "These people are Jews; they are Gypsies; they are Jehovah Witnesses. Some were trade unionists, Communists and homosexuals." He went on with the litany, identifying various groups that had been placed in this camp by the Nazis, and I submit to you that in my judgment, the Nazis were saying in essence, "They are not good enough; therefore they should be terminated, murdered."

As a soldier, I had seen death and dying but nothing like this. I needed to know more, so I walked about the camp. I was taken to barracks where the prisoners had to sleep. I opened the door and stepped across the threshold, but I could go no further. The odor and the stench that comes from death and human waste were overwhelming. I stood there holding my breath.

I knew I had to leave, so I turned toward the door, but before I left I could take a step, I looked down. There, on a bottom bunk near the door, was a man, an emaciated human being of skin and bone. He was on a bed of filthy straw and rags. He was trying desperately to look up at me with that skeletal face and those deep-set eyes, but he was too weak. He had been starved for such a long time. Finally he looked up at me. He said nothing, nor did I. I opened the door, stepped across the threshold and closed the door.

At another building, I was told that I would find all parts of the human anatomy in jars of formaldehyde. This was when I became aware that the Nazis had done medical experiments on human beings at Buchenwald. When the doctors finished their surgeries, they would place those parts of the human anatomy they wished to keep in labeled jars. I could not read the German, but I could see. I saw it all. There were eyes, ears, fingers, hearts, livers, kidneys, genitalia and other parts not labeled.

On a table nearby, I saw human skin. Someone had painted something on the skin. There was a lampshade in the room, and it too had been made out of human skin. The sight was staggeringly repulsive. I think one of the most horrible things that day was realizing that this camp wasn't a singular place. There were others like it all over Germany, and on that day, some of those camps were still in operation. The things that I saw that had been done to people might still be happening in other parts of Germany even while I stood there.

I arrived at another building where the Nazis had interrogated and tortured their prisoners. I found it hard to believe anyone would torture someone else in 1945 in a civilized country like Germany. I saw the blackened blood on the cement floor and the slabs where the victims were placed. On the wall, some of the instruments of torture were still hanging. As I looked at these things I began to understand that some people could do evil things like this to others. Prior to my seeing all of this, I would not have believed that any human being could torture another human being in such a way, but there I became a believer.

I had been in the camp for approximately 4 hours, and in that time I never saw any children. When I asked the young man of their whereabouts, he said, "They are in the camp." As I was leaving this building, I saw the clothing of little children, little children who did not survive. Against one wall, I saw mounds of clothing. There were caps, sweaters, stockings, shoes and baby booties. I saw all of these things and more that belonged to the little children, but I never saw a child.

Finally, I walked past the dead and those who were dying and arrived at another building. As I got close, I could see the dead bodies. They were stacked about four feet high and five feet wide against a building called the crematorium. I went inside, and I discovered six ovens. I walked over and looked into one, and I saw what was left there. I saw a man's blackened skull, his rib cage, the bones and the ashes. The young man said that on a given day the Nazis came with a truck and collected the ashes and spread it on a farm as fertilizer. They used the ashes of the people they killed to grow food to feed their army.

At this point, I knew that I had seen enough, more than I would care to write about at this time. My stomach was churning, and I needed fresh air, so I walked away from my friends. I went back to the gate and waited there for my friends to come. As I waited, I realized that I was not the same any more. Something had happened to me. When I entered the Buchenwald Concentration Camp, I was an angry young black soldier. I was angry at my country for what it was doing to me and my race, but now I could see a bit more clearly. My blinders had come off. My tunnel vision had broadened. I now understood that human suffering was not relegated to just me. Pain and suffering is universal; it can touch all of us.

I also knew on this spring day in April at the Buchenwald Concentration Camp that I had seen the face of evil. I am speaking of racism, anti-Semitism, bigotry and prejudice and all manner of hatred. I saw it all in that camp in Nazi Germany, and they had replicated it throughout Europe and Russia. The Nazis had raised their hatred to another level, but it was that same hate that I had experienced during my tour of duty in my own country. All of this made me know that something had to be done to eradicate this evil. At the time, I did not know what I could do. I was just a 20-year-old soldier, but I had a feeling deep down inside of me that made me know I would do something to help change things when I got home.

When I got home I learned the statistics: twelve million people; about six million Jews were killed. They weren't soldiers. They were the old, the young, the babies, the handicapped, the blind. They were taken out of institutions and injected with poisons because the Nazis said they were not good enough.

That day at Buchenwald I knew I had a reason for being in the Army. I knew I had something to fight for. I kept saying to myself, "Leon, when you get home, you are going to have to do something. You are going to have to make things better." At the end of the day we left that place in silence. None of us spoke about what we had seen.

It wasn't possible to close the camp and move those people on the day that they were liberated, so the army attempted to make things as livable there as possible in the next few weeks and months. My battalion had a water purification section, and many of the men were in and out of the camp as they purified the water. President Dwight Eisenhower sent out a command. He wanted as many of the residents from the area as possible to see what had gone on right under their noses. The townspeople were escorted through every day, usually not voluntarily.

But even though many people in my battalion saw the camp I never heard anyone speak about it. We had all seen unspeakable horror, and I did could not talk of it for more than 25 years. My parents died never knowing of my experience in Buchenwald, but what I witnessed there made me know I did have something to fight for.

GOOD ENOUGH

★CHAPTER FIVE★
FROM EUROPE TO THE PHILIPPINES

Shortly after my experience with the horror of the Buchenwald Concentration Camp, the war against Germany ended. For a few months I was able to see much of Germany, and I enjoyed the beauty of the country even though there was devastation everywhere. Our next orders took us back to France to a staging area in Marseille, France. Our battalion was no longer needed, so it was disbanded. The men of the battalion were sent to a variety of service units. I was assigned to the 1364 Dump Truck Company as one of many soldiers being sent to the Philippines. Our ship traveled through the Panama Canal, which was an educational experience. I marveled at the engineering feat that made it possible for such large vessels to travel from the Atlantic Ocean to the Pacific Ocean in such a short time.

Our ship was only 3 days on the other side of the Panama Canal when atomic bombs were dropped on Nagasaki and Hiroshima in Japan. This made me hope that the ship might return to the United States, but that did not happen. The United States Navy took us ashore in one of their landing crafts and then to our final destination, which was a bombed out convent on Santa Mesa Boulevard outside the city of Manila. My stay in the Philippines lasted approximately 7 boring, uneventful months. The weather was either wet or dry. During the wet season it was muddy, and during the dry season it was dusty.

I learned to type in Manila; the sergeant needed a company clerk, and I was assigned. When I told him I didn't know how to type, his only answer was, "Well, you can learn," and I did. It took a long time, hunting and pecking at the keys. Particularly because every time you made a mistake you had to take out the paper and start over again.

Another new experience in Manila was the dances. You had to buy a ticket in order to dance with the ladies at the dance club.

Another thing I learned about in Manila was the black market. Everything seemed to be for sale there. Even the officers were selling things. I had opportunities to sell things, too, but I never did. I knew if I got caught and got in trouble what it would do to my mother.

The long awaited surrender of the nation of Japan did little to relieve my boredom. There was not much to do for a dump truck company in Manila, but I had to make the most of it, so I made the effort to find some recreational activities. For the first time in my life, I went to hear a symphony and enjoyed it immensely. On another occasion, I attended an opera entitled *Lucia de Lamamoor.* It was intriguing to watch an Italian opera set in Scotland with Filipinos dressed in kilts singing in Italian.

While my experiences in the Philippines were sometimes boring and unpleasant, something positive and unexpected did happen. At the Third Army Headquarters in Calais, France, Order Number 26 was issued. It stated that the soldiers of the 183rd Engineer Combat Battalion were to receive three Bronze Stars: a Bronze Star for participation in the Rhineland Campaign, a Bronze Star for participation in the Ardennes Campaign and a Bronze Star for participation in the Central Europe Campaign. This unexpected recognition of services rendered by black soldiers on the battlefields of Europe was both rewarding and gratifying.

Another reason for my euphoria at this time was the issuing of "demobilization orders for the convenience of the government." Soldiers were to be discharged from the military and sent home. The schedule for separation was determined by the length of service in the military, length of overseas service and the number of citations received. Based on those criteria, points were assigned. My point count was 52, which meant that I could go home in January of 1946. It was one of the premier days in my young life. All my hopes and dreams became a reality as I traveled to the port of embarkation in Manila. Of all the journeys I had ever made while in the army, this one, taking me home, was the longest. The days seemed to get longer and longer as I watched the horizon each morning. Finally I saw on that horizon the shores of California and the Port of Wilmington. What a day that was for me! I made it home on my birthday, January 23, 1946, without any injuries. What a birthday present!

I flew out of Burbank, California, to Fort Meade in Baltimore, Maryland. The processing of my honorable discharge from the United States Army "for the convenience of the government" was completed in 2 days. During my absence, my parents had moved from Philadelphia to Darby Township in Delaware County. I took a taxicab to reach my new home, and when I saw my parents after almost 3 years, there was a very emotional reunion. I reveled in knowing that I was once more at home, and I had left behind me all of the death and dying.

In just a few months, all four of my brothers came home. Two of us had served in the army, two in the Navy and one in the Merchant Marines.

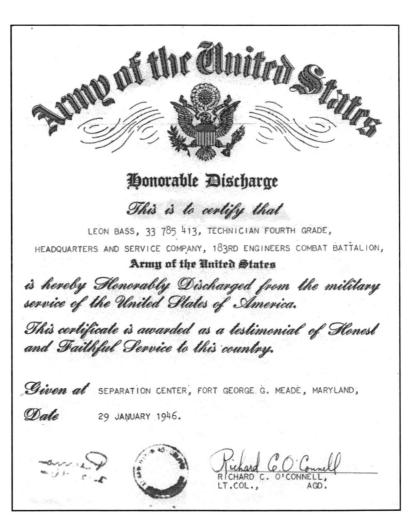

23 4289-1

ENLISTED RECORD AND REPORT OF SEPARATION
HONORABLE DISCHARGE

1. LAST NAME - FIRST NAME - MIDDLE INITIAL	2. ARMY SERIAL NO.	3. GRADE	4. ARM OR SERVICE	5. COMPONENT
BASS LEON	33 785 413	TEC 4	CE	AUS
6. ORGANIZATION	7. DATE OF SEPARATION	8. PLACE OF SEPARATION CENTER		
HQ & SV CO 183RD ENGR C BN	29 JAN 46	FT GEORGE G MEADE MD		
9. PERMANENT ADDRESS FOR MAILING PURPOSES		10. DATE OF BIRTH	11. PLACE OF BIRTH	
129 WALTER AVE FOLCROFT DARBY CO PENN		23 JUN 25	PHILA PA	

12. ADDRESS FROM WHICH EMPLOYMENT WILL BE SOUGHT	13. COLOR EYES	14. COLOR HAIR	15. HEIGHT	16. WEIGHT	17. NO. DEPEND
SEE 9	BROWN	BLACK	5'11½"	180	1

18. RACE	19. MARITAL STATUS	20. U.S. CITIZEN	21. CIVILIAN OCCUPATION AND NO.
WHITE X NEGRO OTHER (specify)	SINGLE X MARRIED OTHER (specify)	YES X NO	STUDENT HIGH SCH VOCATIONAL X-02

MILITARY HISTORY

22. DATE OF INDUCTION	23. DATE OF ENLISTMENT	24. DATE OF ENTRY INTO ACTIVE SERVICE	25. PLACE OF ENTRY INTO SERVICE
15 JUN 43		15 JUN 43	PHILA PA

26. SELECTIVE SERVICE DATA	27. LOCAL S.S. BOARD NO.	28. COUNTY AND STATE	29. HOME ADDRESS AT TIME OF ENTRY INTO SERVICE
YES X NO	25	PHILA CO PA	SEE 9

30. MILITARY OCCUPATIONAL SPECIALTY AND NO.	31. MILITARY QUALIFICATION AND DATE (i.e., Infantry, aviation and marksmanship badges, etc.)
COMPANY CLERK 405	EX M1 RIFLE

32. BATTLES AND CAMPAIGNS
ARDENNES   RHINELAND   CENTRAL EUROPE

33. DECORATIONS AND CITATIONS PHILIPPINE LIBERATION RIBBON WORLD WAR II VICTORY RIBBON
GOOD CONDUCT MEDAL   AMERICAN THEATER RIBBON EUROPEAN AFRICAN MIDDLE
EASTERN SERVICE RIBBON ASIATIC PACIFIC THEATER RIBBON

34. WOUNDS RECEIVED IN ACTION
NONE

35. LATEST IMMUNIZATION DATES				36.	37. SERVICE OUTSIDE CONTINENTAL U.S. AND RETURN		
SMALLPOX	TYPHOID	TETANUS	OTHER		DATE OF DEPARTURE	DESTINATION	DATE OF ARRIVAL
AUG 45	AUG 45	MAY 44	CHOL JUL 45 TYPH DEC 45		4 OCT 44	ENGLAND	12 OCT 44
					4 JAN 46	UNITED STATES	22 JAN 46

38. TOTAL LENGTH OF SERVICE				39. HIGHEST GRADE HELD
CONTINENTAL SERVICE		FOREIGN SERVICE		
YEARS	MONTHS	DAYS	YEARS	MONTHS	DAYS	
1	3	26	1	3	19	TEC 4

39. PRIOR SERVICE
NONE

for convenience a certificate of eligibility No. 3976204 has been
issued by the Veterans Administration to be used for the future request of

40. REASON AND AUTHORITY FOR SEPARATION any gratuity or insurance benefit under title III of the servicemen's read
CONVENIENCE OF THE GOVERNMENT RR 1-1 (DEMOBILIZATION) AR615-365 15 DEC 44

41. SERVICE SCHOOLS ATTENDED
NONE

	EDUCATION (Years)
whem this separation paper was issued VA RO Phila.	4 3

PAY DATA

42. LONGEVITY FOR PAY PURPOSES	43. MUSTERING OUT PAY		44. SOLDIER DEPOSITS	45. TRAVEL PAY	46. TOTAL AMOUNT, NAME OF DISBURSING OFFICER	
YEARS	MONTHS	DAYS	TOTAL	THIS PAYMENT				
2	7	5	$200.00	$100.00	NONE	$5.75	$359.39 PEARSON CAPT FD

INSURANCE NOTICE

IMPORTANT IF PREMIUM IS NOT PAID WHEN DUE OR WITHIN THIRTY-ONE DAYS THEREAFTER, INSURANCE WILL LAPSE. MAKE CHECKS OR MONEY ORDERS PAYABLE TO THE TREASURER OF THE U. S. AND FORWARD TO COLLECTIONS SUBDIVISION, VETERANS ADMINISTRATION, WASHINGTON 25, D.C.

48. KIND OF INSURANCE	49. HOW PAID	50. Effective Date of Allotment Discontinuance	51. Date of Next Premium Due	52. PREMIUM DUE	53. INTENTION OF VETERAN TO
Nat. Serv. U.S. Govt. Conv. Allotment Direct to Collector	X	31 JAN 46	28 FEB 46	$6.40	Continue Continue Only Discontinue X

54. REMARKS (This space for completion of above items or entry of other items specified in W.D. Directives)
LAPEL BUTTON ISSUED   NO DAYS LOST
ASR SCORE 53

APPLICATION FOR
READJUST 107 #3
PASS
STATE Penna
DATE 2-2-46

55. SIGNATURE OF PERSON BEING SEPARATED	56. PERSONNEL OFFICER (Type name, grade and organization - signature)
Leon Bass	VIOLA PAVIC 1ST LT WAC Viola Pavic

WD AGO FORM 53 - 55   This form supersedes all previous editions of

GOOD ENOUGH

★ CHAPTER SIX ★
COLLEGE DAYS

It was 1946, I was 21 years of age and I had spent close to 3 years in the military. Now the critical questions I had to find answers to were "What do I do now? How am I going to make up for lost time?" My parents had always stressed education beyond high school, but that required money, which I did not have. Fortunately, the Congress of the United States had anticipated the needs of the soldiers who had done so much to keep our country safe and secure. In its wisdom, they created and passed legislation called the *G.I. Bill of Rights.* This bill stated that any soldier who had been honorably discharged from the military was entitled to certain benefits. One of those benefits was the right to a college education. The *G.I. Bill* would pay for tuition, books and other equipment and provide a monthly stipend. This bill, in my opinion, was a form of "affirmative action" long before "affirmative action" became controversial.

Temple University had a testing program for soldiers entitled to the *G.I. Bill.* This test was to determine their ability to succeed in college. On the day before I was to take the test, I had been out of town; I'd gone up to Boston to visit the sister of an Army buddy. We'd had a very good time, but I'd been up all night, and I was very tired. I took the exam anyway, and halfway through the exam, I fell asleep. A counselor, on reviewing my test results, said that I might be able to do college work with effort, but not at Temple University.

This rejection did not dissuade me from pursuing admission to another educational institution. It did, however, make me apprehensive when I applied to what was then called West Chester State Teachers College (now West Chester University) in West Chester, Pennsylvania. Very few blacks attended school there; my first year I never saw any black men, although there were more and more each year because of the *G.I. Bill*. In the summer of 1946 I received my letter of acceptance to WCSTC. I was anxious to get started and didn't want to wait until September to enroll, so on good advice from a friend, I enrolled in the summer classes to make certain that I would be accepted again for the fall term.

But my first experience at the college wasn't very positive. I was told that I couldn't live in the dormitory because I was black. After everything I had experienced in the Army, to be told one more time that I wasn't good enough felt like the straw had broken the camel's back. My joy at becoming a college student was diminished even further as I began to attend college in West Chester and learned almost daily that the evil of racism was not restricted to the college campus; it took many forms throughout the town.

The college administration and the townspeople were letting me know that I was not good enough to be accepted in certain prescribed areas of either the college or the town. To say I was angry at these rejections would be an understatement. I was furious at this racist treatment, and at this time I had not yet prescribed to the philosophy of nonviolence.

My father wanted to make sure that I did not do something to jeopardize my status as a college student. When I was at home and complained to him, he said very emphatically, "Don't you go out to that West Chester running your mouth, thinking you alone can change the world. You have one purpose when you go there. That's to get an education. Once you get that, no one can take it away from you.

I listened to my father; I swallowed my pride; I kept my anger and pain inside, and I got my education. But it was at this point in my young life that I understood what James Baldwin meant when he said, "To be black and in America is to be in a constant state of rage."

Despite my father's warning, one day my anger took me up High Street in West Chester to the Warner Theatre. I presented my ticket to the usher, and he directed me to stairs that led up to the balcony where blacks were required to sit. One more time, someone was telling me that I was not good enough to sit down on the main floor with the white patrons. He never should have done that, because I had had more than enough of this racism. I walked past him and took a seat in the middle of the theatre's main floor. This was my protest. I was telling him and everyone else that I was good enough. There are times when you respond to a given situation without thinking of the consequences, but when you do think about what you have done, the nerves take over. I said to myself, "Leon, you are not going to graduate from college; you are going to jail."

The movie ended. People got up to leave, and so did I. As I walked out, I looked to my right and to my left. I was certain "the man" was going to put the arm on me, but it didn't happen. I walked back to my room in town, and with every step I grew taller and taller. In my mind, I was ten feet tall. I was proud because I had confronted the evil oppressor without taking on the violent tactics of that oppressor. This was one of the most difficult things I had ever done in my young life. When you do what is right the feeling *is* exhilarating.

Another unpleasant event took place during that summer of 1946. It occurred during a boat ride from Philadelphia on the Wilson Line. I went on a college-sponsored excursion to enjoy a ride on the river to Wilmington, Delaware.

We left the college on several buses, which took us to Delaware Avenue where the Wilson Line had docked. At the end of the boat trip the buses would meet us there for our return to the college. The Wilson Line provided refreshments and music for dancing as we cruised down the river. All was going smoothly until I decided to dance with one of the coeds. Suddenly a huge man with a blackjack in his back pocket tapped me on my shoulder. He told me that I had to leave the dance floor. I tried to explain that we were a part of the student group from West Chester, but his response was "Niggers are not allowed on the dance floor."

I left the dance floor and proceeded to look for the Dean of Women who was the chaperone on this trip. I told her what had happened on the dance floor. She began to look for the ship's captain, who, she was told, was on the bridge. She proceeded to climb the steps leading to the ship's bridge, but before she could go very far, a loud booming voice yelled, "Get the hell off of my bridge!" The captain's incivility was heard by nearly everyone aboard the boat. The incident cast a pall over the rest of the trip, especially for the black students. Episodes like this confirmed for me that racism is not relegated to the Deep South in our country, but was pervasive throughout the entire United States.

★ CHAPTER SEVEN ★
LOVE AND MARRIAGE

One of the most important events in my life took place that September of 1946. As I approached the college on registration day, I saw a young coed walking toward me. She was a beautiful young lady with a beautiful figure. We both smiled as we passed each other. Needless to say, I turned and took that second look. The next day, I found her sitting with her friends on campus. We looked at one another, and something clicked. From that point on, we would meet on campus each day until our friends figured out that we had become "an item." Her name was Mary Katherine Sullivan, and she was a graduate of the Philadelphia High School for Girls. Mary and a friend had lived in the town of West Chester at the home of a black dentist and his wife, but they moved into the campus dormitory when the college administration was directed by the state to end their discriminatory housing policy.

During the summers, I would attend summer school in order to enable me to complete my education in 3 years instead of 4. While attending summer school I had to secure housing in the town for the 3 summer months. I found a room to rent, however, the landlady told me that I would have to leave when the girls who roomed there during the regular school year returned to school in September. Another woman where I had been boarding heard of my plight, and she convinced the landlady that I was a gentleman who could be trusted in her home with her young girls. When I told Mary about it she just laughed.

During the summer, I would leave West Chester for a weekend at home in Folcroft, Pennsylvania. Each

Mary

Saturday, Mary and I would go to a movie, a dance or go bowling with friends. When we returned to Mary's home, the dining room table would be filled with food and drinks. Mary's grandmother would always have a sumptuous spread prepared for us to eat.

Little did we know that our meeting on that September day would turn into 53 years of marriage. We were married on Saturday, October 16, 1948, at Mary's home with my parents, my brothers and Mary's grandmother present. One day later, on Sunday, we returned to the college. Mary went to her room in the college dormitory, and I went to my rented room in the town of West Chester. In a few weeks, the college administration asked Mary to leave the dormitory because she was a married woman, so of course she came uptown to live with me.

A few months after our marriage Mary's grandmother died. When she died, I realized that her support of our marriage before graduation was predicated on her awareness of her impending death. She did not want her granddaughter to face the problems and difficulties of this world alone. She knew how much we loved each other, and so she readily endorsed our plans to marry even though we were a year or two from our college graduation.

The adjustment to married life was not easy for us because we were now responsible for the maintenance of Mary's grandmother's three-story house in Philadelphia, where we were living, while at the same time keeping up our grades at the college. During this period, Mary's grieving was deep and extended. Consoling her was difficult, but in spite of her grief, she was able to return to her classes.

GOOD ENOUGH

★ CHAPTER EIGHT ★
STUDENT TEACHING: THE AGONY AND THE ECSTASY

During my senior year, the four other eligible black students and I were not allowed to do our student teaching at the high school in West Chester. The high school had a few black students, but all their teachers were white, so we were required to do our student teaching at an all-black secondary school in Chester, Pennsylvania. We had to make our own arrangements for transportation, so I contacted a student friend of mine who owned a car, and he agreed to transport the five student teachers to Chester for a small fee.

I enjoyed my student teacher training and came to know that teaching was my calling. In spite of the long travel every day to Chester, I was able to earn a place on the Dean's List. This was the first and only time I achieved that goal.

GOOD ENOUGH

In June of 1949, I graduated from West Chester State Teachers College with a B.S. degree in Secondary Education. My major was history with a minor in English. Mary would graduate the following year with a B.S. degree in Elementary Education. I took that and passed the National Teachers Examination as soon as I graduated, and Mary passed hers when she graduated the next year. While she was still finishing college, in September 1949, I received my first teaching assignment, at the General George G. Meade Elementary School located at 19th and Oxford Streets in North Philadelphia. In keeping with the United States Supreme Court's *Plessy v. Ferguson* decision of 1896, which ruled that "separate but equal" was the law of the land, the Meade School was all black — all of the students, teachers and the principal were black.

At that time, the Meade School was the largest elementary school in the state. There were 1,800 pupils in attendance, with the first three grades on half-day sessions. In my fifth grade class, there were 49 pupils on the roll. This was a challenge for a first year teacher, especially since there were few teaching materials on hand. My situation was ameliorated by kind, experienced colleagues who provided assistance and the basic teaching needs. The children were mostly cooperative and progressed well under my supervision, but many of them lived in substandard housing. The buildings they lived in were three stories high with three apartments on each floor. For most, central heating was either not available or not in working condition. Each floor had only one bathroom, which was used by two families. It was amazing to me how many students were able to come to school clean and neat despite these circumstances.

I wanted to make my health lessons as meaningful as possible, but it was difficult to teach the children about experiences some of them had never had. Showers were foreign to many of them, and in some cases I am certain that bathtubs were not usable. However, I found a way to give them an awareness of what they might encounter as they grew older. In the basement of our school there were two small gymnasiums, one for boys and one for girls, and there were showers that I could use with parental consent. I found that some children had experienced showering at the home of a friend or relative, but most had not. I took the class down to see the shower rooms where we discussed how to use them and other basic showering needs. For example, each girl would need a shower cap, and I also had them bring soap, body lotions and towels. A day for showers was scheduled weekly, and the students excitedly looked forward to this new experience. The parents responded positively to the plan, and that had a salutary effect on the students and on me.

I consulted the principal about having one of the female custodians escort the girls into the shower room. She readily agreed to help me in this new venture. In the beginning, the boys were excited but fearful about entering the showers, but once they got started, it was hard to get them out. I continued those health lessons throughout my stay as a fifth grade teacher at the school. I taught at the school for 14 years, from 1949 to 1963.

One of my best lessons resulted from the federal government distributing bushel baskets of apples to the schools in certain neighborhoods. My class enjoyed eating the apples, but once they finished, they also enjoyed throwing them at each other. This resulted in the principal saying, "No more apples!" Somehow I convinced him that my class would put their apples to better use. With his permission, I began a lesson that involved arithmetic. First, I asked the class, "Do you like apple pie?" This brought forth from them a chorus of "Yes!" My next question was, "Have you ever baked an apple pie?"

Only a few had ever done so. With this information, I posed the question I already knew the answer to: "Would you like to bake some apple pies?" The response was a resounding "Yes!" My experience in pie baking was nil, but I did my research. Mary gave me a recipe, the students purchased all the necessary ingredients and we set aside a time for preparing and baking pies. After thoroughly washing their hands and sanitizing a table, the girls put on their hair nets, and both boys and girls put on their aprons. Next, we had to decide on the number of pies needed and the size of each slice. This required the use of fractions to make enough to accommodate 50 pupils and a few extra for hungry friends. The flour, sugar, butter, apples and other ingredients had to be measured according to the recipe and the size of our pie pans. As the aroma of our first pies began to permeate the third floor hallway, I was besieged with requests for some of what we were baking. Sharing would come only after all members of my class were served. This meant that only a few teachers could taste what turned out to be the best dessert one could imagine.

Taking showers and baking pies made the teaching of health and arithmetic come alive for my students. It also made teaching at the elementary level a most rewarding experience for me.

★ CHAPTER NINE ★
THERE'S NO PLACE LIKE HOME

Each day during my first year of teaching, I would walk a few blocks to Temple University where I pursued a master's degree in Elementary Education. This was the time that Mary and I called "our lean years." My salary was only $2,200 a year, hardly enough to maintain Mary's last year at college and our living in Mary's grandmother's old 13-room row house in North Philadelphia. We had to budget very carefully. Quite often my evening meal after class at Temple University was taken at a restaurant in a hotel owned and operated by the famous Father Divine.

Father Divine was a controversial figure in Philadelphia; he had been well-known as a preacher throughout the South and in New York City for several decades before coming to Philadelphia in the 1940s. The meals at his Loraine Hotel, located on Broad Street at Fairmount Avenue in North Philadelphia, were a real bargain at 25 cents. The food was excellent, and the portions were substantial. For all who had enjoyed a good meal, it was expected as each was leaving to show appreciation by saying, "Thank you, Father."

Mary and I had planned to wait 3 years before having children so that both of us would be tenured and our jobs secured, but the 3 years turned out to be 6 years. During this period my father died. His passing was devastating for all of the family. Dad was a gentle giant of a man in my eyes, for he did so many things, and he did them well. He, along with my mother, made all of us children feel secure and happy. Everyone who knew him respected him because he respected all people no matter who or what they were.

On one occasion after my father died my brother and I went into a "Mom and Pop" grocery store where the storeowner told us how sorry he was to hear about our father's death. He said that our dad was a caring and kind person. He told us about the day my dad came into his store and saw a woman crying at the counter and wanted to know what her problem was.

The owner said to us, "I told your dad that the woman had been coming to the store for weeks asking for food to feed her children, but she had no money to pay for the food. I had to tell her that I could no longer give her food without some payment for what she already owed me. Your father took me aside and told me, 'Whenever this woman comes to your store asking for food, you give her whatever she wants, and I will pay the bill,' and your father's only request of me was, 'Don't tell her what I am doing.' That woman and her children had food to eat for a year and a half and never knew of her benefactor."

My father's legacy of love has been a large part of my daily struggle to be a better person. I had been teaching for several years and was feeling good about my development and my classroom successes. However, despite the progress and good times in the classroom, when my students left school they were often involved in arguments and fights. Many had learned that violence was the only way to resolve their disagreements. I wanted to change that behavior, but it was a very difficult task for me, and I was in a quandary as to what I could do.

★ ★ ★

In 1954, Mary had a nervous breakdown. We never were able to discover the cause of her illness even though we consulted several doctors. Several of them recommended electric shock treatments, which we tried, and they seemed to help but gave her only short-term relief. It was an old medical practitioner who gave us the answer to our problem. He asked, "How long have you been married?" We told him it had been 6 years. He then said, "Have a baby." We followed his advice, and in 2 weeks Mary was pregnant, and in time her nervous condition resolved.

Leon, Jr., was born on March 11, 1955. This was the most joyous moment of our married life, but it also made us aware of the many responsibilities that came with an addition to the family. We brought our son home from the University of Pennsylvania Hospital, and then we realized how little we knew. How do we change diapers? How do we bathe him? How do we get him to stop crying? I will never forget how I walked the floor holding him, hoping he would stop the crying and go to sleep. A week later we visited our pediatrician who told us that the baby's formula was not providing him the nourishment he needed. It was amazing how quiet Leon became after he started receiving his new formula. He even slept through the night!

Leon, Jr. was just 4 years of age when our daughter, Delia Marie, was born on November 4, 1959. While Leon, Jr. was quiet and reserved, Delia was loquacious and outgoing. Despite these differences, they bonded and remain in a close relationship even today. Whatever Leon would do, Delia was determined to follow. She was a tomboy and could outrun most of the boys in the neighborhood and in her elementary school.

As mentioned previously, our country, in its wisdom, had passed what is called the *G.I. Bill of Rights,* which made it possible for men and women who had served their country during World War II to get an education and to secure decent, affordable housing.

In the early 1950s, Mary and I made efforts to find a home away from the inner city. This became a real struggle for us because white society was not amenable to having people of color living in "their" neighborhoods. We searched for almost a year, and it seemed that there was no place available to us. Some salesmen, if they saw us coming, would go out the back door rather than offer some flimsy reason why they could not sell to us. There were others who were quite candid and would say, "We are not selling to Negroes." They could get away with this because, although open housing laws had been passed, they were not being enforced.

We traveled across Philadelphia into Montgomery and Bucks Counties only to be rejected at every turn. When we were almost ready to give up on our search, my brother told me that in a Bucks County town called Trevose, a development named *Concord Park* had been built. Included in their advertisement was the term "open housing." So we made our journey to Concord Park and found that it was as advertised. The literature was clear that they were selling to all who were seeking a new home. The homes were ranch-style dwellings that included three bedrooms, bath, a living room, dining area and closets in each bedroom and hallway. There was also additional storage space in an attic accessible by a ladder and a one-car garage, which had a door leading into the house. The property was one-quarter acre, and there was no question in our minds that this was just what we had been looking for. The price was right for us, and the *GI Bill* helped to make it affordable.

On the day we moved in, our white next-door neighbors came over to greet us. As we settled in and the development grew in population, we began to see the kind of diversity that was rarely seen in other neighborhoods. There were blacks, whites, Asians and Latinos. We soon came to know some who were homosexual, and realized that various religions were represented, too. I discovered that members of the Society of Friends were instrumental in the development of this diverse community by helping to finance the purchase of the land and all that was required to turn farm land into this housing development.

Those who moved into Concord Park were young families with children from infants to pre-teens. This was just what we wanted — to have our children live and play and grow in such a diverse environment. Many of the families were what might be considered middle class. They were teachers, students, small business owners, mechanics, nurses, salesmen and social workers.

I met and became friends with some families who were members of the Society of Friends. I knew very little about their religious practices but readily accepted an invitation to their meeting one Sunday. After this visit, we attended for more than 3 years. I knew I had found a philosophy that I could live by — the belief that "There is that of God in every person, and He or She is with us daily." The members of this meeting in time became part of my extended family.

★ ★ ★

While teaching in the School District of Philadelphia, I found it necessary to find employment during the summer recess. Teachers received salary only during the months of September through June but not during the summer hiatus. Fortunately, I usually found employment with the Philadelphia Department of Recreation, but by 1964 just after the March on Washington, I was not looking forward to those hot summer days as a recreational leader. The possibility of violence was ever present on my mind because I knew that gangs often settled their disputes on the city's playgrounds.

Each summer, I had been approached by a friend who lived in our community and was a member of the American Friends Service Committee (AFSC) who wanted me to lead one of their summer work camps. Every year, the AFSC would set up work camps in various communities across the United States. Each time she asked if I would provide the leadership for one of these camps, I refused. But finally one summer, Mary and I acquiesced.

We packed our car the day before I closed my school for the vacation period. When I arrived home, we put our two children, Leon, Jr. and Delia in the car and left for Brunswick, Maine. I drove all night, and we reached our destination as dawn was breaking.

Our sleeping accommodations were in the front room of a fraternity house on the Bowdoin College campus, a two-story building that could accommodate all of the 24 young campers who would arrive the next day. These campers, who would come from different regions of the United States, had to pay to participate in this summer service experience.

The next day, a representative from the AFSC, stationed in Brunswick, Maine, spoke to us about our tasks in this affluent college community. She said our work would entail the building of a playground on the outskirts of town, and we were to transform a town dump where all kinds of refuse had been discarded. The main goal of this project was to bring together the people of the lower economic area of Brunswick (Moodyville) and the more affluent people of the college town of Brunswick.

Our first step, after getting acquainted with each other, was to begin the planning stage. This required visiting the work site and determining what sort of playground equipment could be created there. Resources were needed, such as lumber, nails, saws and a host of other tools, equipment and supplies. To solve our transportation problem, a school bus had been provided. This would be my first attempt at driving a large vehicle, but after a few practice sessions, I finally became a competent bus driver.

Our first introduction to solving problems by consensus (a *Society of Friends* tradition) took place during our planning sessions. We spent many hours trying this process, but I am sorry to say we were not successful in resolution by consensus.

While I supervised the construction of the playground, Mary was overseeing the cooking and cleaning back at our living quarters. A schedule was made so that everyone shared in all phases of the work to be done, including preparing three meals daily. I marveled at the way Mary kept track of all our expenses.

Being responsible for the welfare of 24 teenagers created some headaches. The combination of parenting our two young children, as well as the other unfamiliar teens with a variety of personalities, was particularly difficult, and we looked forward to the day when the project would be completed. As we were reaching the end of our work camp, we evaluated what we had done. Did we accomplish our goals? Had we completed our mission? Our physical accomplishments could easily be seen. They were: two large latrines, a basketball court, one tree house, seesaws for four, balance beams for two and swings for two.

We were especially pleased to see how 24 strangers, over the course of the summer, became friends, and I was amazed to see how a very diverse group from different religious, racial and socioeconomic backgrounds were able to work together to complete a rather difficult project.

Mary totaled our expenses and discovered that we had a small surplus. So she made the suggestion that we go to a restaurant and treat the campers and ourselves to a lobster feast. On the night of our campers' departure, tears were overflowing. As difficult as our task had been, we remembered this adventure as a wonderful learning experience never to be forgotten. Our report to the AFSC was submitted, and it received an excellent rating. We were told that our work camp was the best of all the camps during the summer of 1965.

Several years later in September of 1972, Leon, Jr., who attended Cornell University, drove up to Brunswick, Maine. He found that the playground was still being used by the Moodyville community under the auspices of the YMCA.

★ CHAPTER TEN ★
MY HERO, DR. MARTIN LUTHER KING

A ray of hope came when the clarion voice of Dr. Martin Luther King came out of the Deep South. Dr. King proclaimed that love and nonviolence were ways to achieve equality and justice. This new philosophy of hope had its beginning when Rosa Parks, a black seamstress, left her job in 1955 and boarded a bus for the ride home. Rosa was tired but courageous when she took a seat in the front section of the bus. The bus driver saw her and demanded that she get up from her seat so that a white man could sit down.

Rosa smiled and said, "No."

The driver became livid and told her that he would have her arrested if she did not move.

Again, Rosa said, "No."

The driver called the police, who came and arrested that God-fearing woman. She was taken to jail and booked. The news of Rosa's arrest spread all across the city of Montgomery, Alabama. The black citizens were outraged at the injustice perpetrated against Sister Rosa, and they congregated in their churches in great numbers to discuss the problem. After much debate and discussion, it was decided that all Montgomery blacks would boycott the bus company.

Hearing about Rosa Parks made me remember my own experience on a bus in Mississippi. I could see the difference between her experience and mine; for me there would have been no quarter. I would have been beaten and jailed. But the Rosa Parks incident came later, after the war and after Martin Luther King had begun to be heard talking about non-violence.

Because of this, I don't think that Rosa Parks had the same fear that I had. She didn't feel she was by herself, the way that I did that day in Mississippi. She was a part of the NAACP. They had arranged for this incident to happen; it wasn't spontaneous. It was a different time and different mindset.

When I heard about Rosa Parks I thought how wonderful it was that she had stood up for herself. She encouraged me and made me realize I could do something to make a change.

This creative nonviolent tactic would create a loss of revenue not only for the bus company, but for many of the city's merchants as well. For 13 long months, the black citizens walked, bearing all of the hardships that came their way. Those who owned automobiles transported those who needed help getting to their jobs. The police of Montgomery used threats and other tactics to try to disrupt the effectiveness of the carpooling, but the black community was united in its resolve. This nonviolent protest was called "The Montgomery Bus Boycott." In the eyes of many, this was the beginning of the Civil Rights Movement in the United States, and The U.S. Supreme Court, in 1956, finally declared segregated seating on buses unconstitutional. The blacks of Montgomery had won, but

Dr. Martin Luther King, Jr. reminded the boycott participants to remain peaceful. He told them to go back to riding the buses and take their seats with dignity. Then he said to all assembled, "We will wear them down with our capacity for love."

I was in Philadelphia teaching school when I read Dr. King's remarks. I thought that Dr. King was out of his mind to be asking me and others to use love and peaceful protest as a tactic to change society. I could not see the wisdom in my loving people who wouldn't hesitate to spit on me, beat me, mistreat my children and bomb our churches. But those in the "movement" listened, believed and accepted his philosophy of nonviolence and love. They believed that the price for them was not too high a price to pay to effectuate the changes needed in their community and across the entire United States.

What did it mean for me? Was the price of "wearing them down with love" too high? No, it was not, but it was still a struggle for me. Although I believed in what Dr. King was saying, I wondered if I had the courage to stand up and do something about it. I felt it was a challenge to me: could I do what he was advocating? It was the right thing to do, but it took courage, and I had to work at it. These events began to impact my life. This new philosophy of love and nonviolence permeated my being and drew me in to become a part of the struggle. I spoke of this new way of solving problems with my students, and we decided to try using conflict resolution. Our progress was slow, but we were making some gains.

During my efforts to teach this new approach to my students, Dr. King visited Philadelphia. He came to a playground on Berks Street, not far from Temple University in North Philadelphia, to speak to the children who lived in that neighborhood. I took my entire class to the playground because we wanted to see and hear this giant of a man. He walked out on the playground, and I scrutinized him carefully. He was just a little guy, only about five foot six inches, but as he began to speak, I recognized him for the giant he truly was. He said things I needed to hear and things my class needed to hear.

He spoke of loving, caring, understanding and showing compassion. He spoke of respecting all people regardless of who or what they were. He spoke directly to the children about striving for excellence in school and in their lives. He said, "If you can't be the pine on the top of the hill, then be the little shrub in the valley below, but be the best no matter where you are."

Then he admonished them when he said, "You might not become a doctor, a lawyer, a teacher or an engineer. Now, some of you might have to sweep the streets; so be it; but if you sweep those streets, I want you to sweep those streets like Beethoven wrote his music; you sweep those streets like Michelangelo painted those pictures; you sweep those streets like Shakespeare wrote his poetry. I want you to be the best, no matter what it is that you do."

I was mesmerized. No one had ever touched me with words the way his words touched me, and I went back to my school with a determination to be a participant in some way in the Civil Rights Movement. It was this motivation that sent me to Washington, DC, with 250,000 other people on August 28, 1963, for the March on Washington for Jobs and Freedom. It was a defining moment of the American Civil Rights Movement. We were there to tell our Congress and the world that we were good enough, and it was time for a change.

Mary stayed home with the children, and I went down to Washington, D.C., on a bus filled with other people going to the march. Buses were heading to DC. from all over the country, and because there were many places where blacks would not be allowed to eat or used the toilet, special stops had been arranged along the way. As we drove down the highway people stood along the streets waving at us.

What a day this was! It was a very hot day, and we stood on the Mall in Washington with thousands and thousands of people. There was happiness everywhere. We all talked to each other whether we knew each other or not.

There were several speakers, including A. Phillip Randolph, the man who had founded the Sleeping Car Porters, a union that my father had belonged to. Because the vast majority of railroad porters were black, they had not been allowed into the railroad unions. Finally, with the help of men like Randolph, the Sleeping Car Porters became a part of the AFL-CIO.

While I was interested in hearing Randolph speak that day in Washington, D.C., I was like everyone else there; I was waiting to hear from this giant of a man, Martin Luther King.

When I say giant, I mean it metaphorically. As I've mentioned before, Dr. King was not a tall man, but he was a giant when he spoke. As he started to speak that day I stood enraptured. I'd heard him speak several times before, and he had always impressed me, but that day was still something special.

I looked around at all the people standing there; they were crying, hugging each other, as they listened to him, and I realized right then just how much this man had been chosen to be the change. Once in a lifetime you meet someone who has that charisma, that ability to move people. All the dying, all the singing, all the crying manifested themselves in the words he spoke that day on the Mall in Washington, D.C. I stood there and listened, and I cried. I knew right then that I was going to be an agent of nonviolent social change. You can't affect change in others if you haven't changed your own self. How can I say I love you to someone who is treating you like dirt? It doesn't just happen; it's a struggle every day, even today. I can't hate them. Instead, I try to remember my mother's statement, "You have to love the unlovable."

Something that I came to know is that when you step out on that platform you have to be prepared for the pain that will come. Is the price too high? You have to think about it, you have to be committed to it and believe it. It was as if Dr. King grabbed me that day and said, "Leon you have to get into the struggle." Changes comes slowly, and it comes daily. You have to work at it, you have to struggle with it. I carried this desire to be an agent for change and social justice back to the all-black school where I was teaching.

My experience that day in Washington, D.C., influenced me in many ways. We had been living in Concord Park, a community founded by the Quakers for several years, and I had gotten to know a number of people of the Quaker faith. One young man often drove into Philadelphia with me, and he had invited Mary and the children and me to attend the Quaker meeting. We had been attending the meeting in South Hampton, Bucks County, for 3 years, but we hadn't come to any conclusion about whether or not we should join.

The day of the March on Washington, Quakers played a big part in organizing the buses and other aspects of the event. I thought about that as I listened to Martin Luther King say that there is God in everybody. I came home and told Mary I thought that it was time we joined the Quakers because they were the people that I had seen who lived their lives closest to that philosophy: there is God in us all.

★ CHAPTER ELEVEN ★
ASSIGNED AS A PRINCIPAL

At the all-black elementary school where I was teaching, I became more aware of the fight that was just beginning against racism in the public schools of Philadelphia. When I first began teaching the standard practice in the Philadelphia school system was that there were two hiring lists for teachers, one list for white teachers and one for black teachers.

While white teachers could teach or become principals in black schools, black teachers could not teach or become principals in white schools. This practice, of course, made it much more difficult for a black teacher to advance, because the number of openings was substantially less.

I began to hear about Floyd Logan soon after becoming a teacher. One of the local activists in the Philadelphia community, Logan had developed an organization; which he called The Educational Equality League; in about 1932. Its primary goal was to bring about racial equality for people of color within the School District of Philadelphia.

Through the efforts of this champion of change, the separate list for placement of black teachers in the schools was discontinued, and opportunities for people of color to become administrators became a reality.

As a young black teacher, I was told by my white principal that it would not be in my best interest to become aligned in any way with The Educational Equality League. This was just one more way to try to discourage and prevent minorities from gaining a foothold in the administration of a school system whose student population was becoming increasingly black.

My first assignment as principal in an all-black elementary school will be forever imprinted in my memory. I remember going out into the school yard one November day to greet the parents of the kindergarten children who were lined up preparing to enter. The faces of those parents were filled with tears, for they had just heard that our President, John F. Kennedy, had been assassinated. The memory of that terrible tragedy comes to mind whenever I speak of my principalship at the Smith Elementary School. This was a good school for a principal's first assignment. It was small and located in a lower middle class community. The students were well-behaved and reflected the good values instilled by their parents. Some of the teachers were quite experienced, and some had only a few years in the classroom. The building was old but had been well-maintained, and the school was one of a very few in lower middle class neighborhoods to have an orchestra.

My daughter, Delia, was attending a Friends school in Bucks County that was predominately white and served an upper class white community. To help promote diversity, I arranged for the two schools to visit one another. We arranged to have some of the parents attend a get acquainted meeting at one of the schools. Their task was to make plans for the host school to prepare activities to share with the visiting school and then have lunch together. To help in greeting one another, we planned for everyone to wear name tags when they came together. The host school's orchestra would play a few songs followed by group singing. A light lunch would be served, and we would close at an agreed upon time. The visiting school would also have an opportunity to host on another occasion. This exchange proved to be a success and continued for several years.

In order to meet the requirements of the 1954 Supreme Court decision *(Brown v. Board of Education)* striking down segregation in public schools, the Philadelphia School Board decided to make changes in its assignment of principals. These changes resulted in my being transferred from my position as principal of the all-black Walter George Smith Elementary School in South Philadelphia to principal of the all-white Edwin Forrest Elementary School in Northeast Philadelphia. When told of my new assignment, I was somewhat conflicted about the change. My years at the all-black school had been very productive and satisfying, but with this new assignment I felt a degree of uncertainty. I had heard that there were some concerns on the part of some parents and teachers at the Forrest School about my coming, and I must admit, this gave me concerns as well.

It was customary for a new principal to be introduced to the faculty and parents by the District Superintendent, but on my first day, the District Superintendent became conveniently ill, and so I was introduced by the outgoing principal. This only added to my concerns about the challenges ahead. But after a few weeks of meeting and greeting the staff, parents and teachers, I knew that there was no need to be concerned about my future as the educational leader at the school. When I visited the students in their classrooms, it was obvious that I had their stamp of approval.

The St. Bernard Parochial School was our neighbor across the street. I soon discovered that a quiet tension existed between some of the teachers at the two schools, although I never understood why. It came to my attention when I invited some of St. Bernard's primary classes to our Christmas program.

In order to accommodate the number of students, I had our students sit two to a seat in the auditorium. All of the children had a wonderful experience enjoying the presentation and getting to know each other. It was only when I overheard some of our teachers complain that our children were being made uncomfortable in order to accommodate our visitors that I felt that tension.

I never spoke of the negative comments I had overheard, and I thanked the entire faculty for their support in bringing the joy of Christmas to all of the lovely children. After that incident, I realized just how important it was to have visited St. Bernard School on my arrival at my new assignment.

I had gone there unannounced to meet the Parish priest. He asked me, "Why are you here?" I responded that I had come to see him. He said, "No one has ever come to see me before." And I replied, "Well, I'm here now." This encounter was the beginning of a good friendship.

At the Forest School, what began with anxiety turned into love. When parents came to the school for the first time and met me, they were often surprised that I was black; their children just never mentioned it.

GOOD ENOUGH

★ ★ ★

In April of 1968 I was in Houston, Texas, for a national Elementary School Principals meeting as one of the representatives for the Philadelphia principals. On the evening of April 4, some of my colleagues and I went to see a game at the Astrodome. While we were sitting and waiting for the game to start the news of Martin Luther King's assassination came on the large stadium screen.

I was surrounded by white people. Many of them stood up and began to applaud. I heard them saying things like "good," and "We got that Son of a bitch."

I got out of there as quickly as I could and went back to my room to watch the television. It was a terrible thing; people felt they had lost the dream because they had lost the dreamer. It took me a long time, 2 or 3 months, to get over my emotional upset at Dr. King's death.

GOOD ENOUGH

★ CHAPTER TWELVE ★
BAPTISM OF FIRE

I enjoyed my 2 and a half years at the Forrest School, and leaving was not easy to do. But while there, I became a member of the Elementary School Principals Council. As one of its delegates, I served on a committee that was concerned with the development of a new salary schedule for principals. We had met with the District Two Superintendent and the Superintendent over all the Philadelphia Schools. During our discussions, we were told that some of the school board members felt that the high school principals' salaries were more than adequate when you consider the help given by their vice-principals. I took issue with this statement even though I was only an elementary principal, and responded by saying, "Any board members who believe that are not well-informed and do not know what they are talking about."

Later, during a break from our discussion, I was called aside by my District Superintendent who informed me that the Superintendent of Schools was interested in securing qualified principals to fill two vacancies in his district. One vacancy was at a large elementary school, and the other was a large, all-male high school. He also wanted to know if I had a secondary school principal's certificate. I told him that I would have my certification in a month. With this in mind, he asked which of the two schools, the Frederick Douglas Elementary School or the Benjamin Franklin High School, would interest me. He wanted to know if I could provide the leadership that these two schools needed. My interest was in the high school even though I knew that it would be a challenge for anyone who took the position at an all-black high school with 2,000 male students, and I knew that before I accepted this offer, I needed time to discuss this opportunity with my family.

Mary didn't want me to go to the new school at first; she was worried about me, but after a long discussion, the children said, "Go for it," Mary agreed, and I felt comfortable about my decision to accept this new position. Militancy was at a peak in that area and in that school. I had just become a Quaker; in Concord Park I had learned to respect their philosophy that God is in every person. My kids were growing up in that society. It wasn't so challenging to be a Quaker at the elementary school. I was going to find it a lot more challenging at Benjamin Franklin High School.

The next day I received a telephone call from my District Superintendent who said to me, "Leon, it's yours. You are to be the new principal of the Benjamin Franklin High School." There was just one catch. He wanted to know if I would be willing to meet with members of the community at a large house in North Philadelphia. I told him I would, and arrangements were made for me to attend this meeting on a Sunday. When I arrived, I recognized some of the people in attendance. The group was approximately 30 in number, and it included parents, students, school counselors, clergy and an assortment of others that I did not know. I was not aware that this was the first time that a community had been involved in the selection of a school principal.

The house where we met had been rehabbed, and the whole first floor was one open room Seats had been arranged around the room in a horseshoe, and at the top of horseshoe was one seat: mine. After introductions were made, the questioning began. They wanted to know where I grew up and the schools I had attended. "Why are you interested in the high school?" I told them that I had had a lot of different experiences in my time, and I thought that I could make a contribution at the high school. I had worked at a number of different schools, and I wanted them to know that I wasn't just jumping into this job unprepared. There was also an interest in the elementary schools where I had served as principal. These were just routine questions that one would expect, but then came the more searching interrogation.

When asked why I wanted to be principal of Franklin High School, my answer was not based on anything I had read in a book, it came from my heart. I told them that my interest was one of service. I felt that I had something to offer the young men at Ben Franklin High School. It would come from my being a positive role model as a parent, as an educator who believes in excellence and as a young black soldier who had served his country in a segregated army.

Then a more demanding question was asked: "What position would you take over a critical issue that had the teachers and the administration on one side and the student body and the community on the other side?" I knew that this question put me between a rock and a hard place, but my answer had to be what I believed to be a valid one. I told them that once I had all the facts, I would make my position clear. It would be based, in my judgment, on what I thought was the right thing to do for the students, the school and the community. I would then accept whatever the consequences might be.

When I answered that question in the way I thought to myself, "Well, it looks like I'm not going to get this school. Leon, you might as well go home." But in the end, they told me that was the question that swayed the people there in my favor. I didn't know there was such unrest at that school that the current principal was going to be gotten rid of. He couldn't cope with the changes. He had done some things that were great, but times had changed.

At one time, Benjamin Franklin High School had been named Central High School, and it catered to talented children. You had to apply for admittance, and it was difficult to get in. But times change, and neighborhoods change. A new school for the gifted was opened at Broad and Olney. It was named Central High School, and all the trophies that had been won were sent up there. They changed the name of the older school to Benjamin Franklin, and it became a comprehensive high school for boys. As the neighborhood changed, there were more poor and homeless in the area and more people on welfare or who needed help in other ways. The changes were reflected in the school as gangs became popular.

One week later, during the early summer of 1968, I was told by my District Superintendent that I would be assigned as principal of the Benjamin Franklin High School. I pondered over this promotion and wondered why I had been given this position of leadership. My tenure was to begin officially in September, but a telephone call from the Assistant Superintendent of Schools informed me that I was to report to the school without delay. I didn't understand that he meant for me to go to the school the very next day, even though I was still officially the principal at Forrest Elementary. When I failed to report the next day as directed I was sternly admonished. When I tried to explain my reasons for not going in that morning, that I still had responsibilities at my current school, he said, "Any reason you give would be unacceptable. Put your present school in the hands of your counselor and report as ordered." This demand really confirmed to me that all was not well at Ben Franklin High School. Being asked to go to the school in June when my official date of assignment was September seemed unusual. I later found that this early arrival was to give me a chance to become aware of the school's many problems.

Franklin High School was considered a difficult school even when I was a young student attending West Philadelphia High School. I became more cognizant of this when I served as a substitute teacher there during the Jewish High Holy Days in 1949. I was just a freshman at West Chester State Teachers College, but the shortage of substitutes was extremely acute, so I was given this very challenging assignment. Now in 1968, the task had become more of a challenge. The students were no longer polite and respectful. Black awareness and other racial issues had made them more assertive and outspoken.

There had been a movement within the school and the community to oust the current principal and appoint a black male to his position, but not all of the students and teachers wanted to see this happen. There was a schism within the school's population around this and other issues. It was into this maelstrom that I was thrown. I had inherited a chaotic, all-black, all-male, urban high school.

My first meeting with the current principal was tense but fairly pleasant. I had met him in 1949 when I served as a substitute teacher at the school, and I had encountered him again in 1963 when I became an elementary school principal and served in the same district in which he was assigned. He extended the courtesy one would expect from a professional educator, but no more than that.

Franklin High School was a seven-story building, and as I arrived that first day I saw students throwing paper out the windows. Gathered in front of the school were hundreds of black and Latino male students, blocking traffic. My first thought was "Why are they not in their classes?" I did not know at the time that many of these students had participated in a large demonstration at the Philadelphia Board of Education building to protest the poor quality of their education and, as I learned later, also to demand assignment of a black principal. The school board had already added a black vice-principal to the two white vice-principals at the school in an attempt to placate some of the students and to help prevent continued racial unrest. However, during the demonstration, things had gotten out of hand, police were called, some students were beaten and others had been arrested.

This was the kind of angry crowd I was confronted with. In order to enter the building, I cautiously started making my way through the crowd. I had almost made it to the door, but a very large student blocked my path.

He asked in a booming voice, "Mister, are you the new dude they made principal here?"

I answered his question in an equally loud voice, "That is what they have been telling me!"

I tried to pass by him, but the students crowded around me and began to fire questions about my plans for the school.

In a very firm voice I said, "Back off! Give me a break; I have just arrived here!"

At this point one of the students responded, "Mister, if you do not do something right away, we are going to burn this school down!"

He was very serious; they were all serious, and I knew that I had my work cut out for me, but finally, I was able to enter the building. I later learned that this demonstration was for my benefit.

I looked around and saw many of the students wearing dashikis; there were gangs, and there were militants. Some of the students were bright and well-informed, but these were not the same breed of youngsters that I had encountered before. They didn't make requests, they made demands. The former principal, raised in a different era, didn't understand these young people.

On this same day some of the students were following a black policeman who had a young man by the scruff of his neck; they were headed toward the gymnasium. The officer was being called "pig" and a few other choice names. When I noticed the principal head back into his office and close the door, I knew I had to intervene. I entered the gymnasium office and spoke with the officer who, by this time, was quite agitated. When I asked if he would allow me to take care of the situation, he readily turned the young man over to me and left the school. I realized that I needed to get involved in this situation immediately if my leadership role as principal was to be respected by the students and staff. I then took the student to the disciplinary office where a vice-principal handled the problem. I was there at the school every day after that until the end of the school year, even though I had not officially taken over the role of principal.

A meeting was held at the end of that first school day, and I was introduced to the faculty and staff. My remarks were brief. I asked for their help during this leadership transition period and let them know that I looked forward to working with them for the benefit of the students. During the remaining few days before the summer break, I toured the seven-story building where it appeared to me that teaching and learning were at a standstill. Many of the students spent their time in the halls or in the stairwells, not in the classroom. Each day I was made more aware of the appalling conditions existing in the school. It became abundantly clear to me that I was totally unprepared for what I was about to encounter.

These students were ready to confront anyone, including the principal, on issues that were important to them. There were people in the community who, in an organized systematic way, were encouraging students to disrupt the teaching process in order to gain a power base within the school. In a short period of time, I discovered, too, that there were also teachers who participated in planning many of the disruptions that took place. Unfortunately, those few unmotivated, uncaring teachers gave students some justification for their attitudes regarding the educational process at Benjamin Franklin High School. While I encouraged student participation in improving the quality of their education, I, of course objected to their methods.

One of my vice-principals informed me that there were approximately 24 gangs within the school, four of them actively engaged in violence. One morning in September as I went out the front entrance of the building, I found myself in the midst of a gang fight. The gang members were using a variety of weapons: bricks, clubs, fists and knives, and I was caught up in all of this violence. Suddenly, I was surrounded by members of the school's security force and ushered back into the building. I was firmly warned that I was never to put myself in harm's way and to always be alert as I moved about the school.

As I walked about, I soon noticed someone following me. He was always close to me wherever I went in the school. When I reported this to the head of security at the school, I was informed that the deputy superintendent has provided a bodyguard for my protection. The bodyguard would meet me when I parked my car at the school each morning and walked with me when I left for home.

The gang activity outside the school increased in intensity until one day it erupted within the building. One of the large elevators descended to the first floor, and when the doors opened, I saw a student at the back of the elevator sitting on the floor. He was holding his stomach and was bleeding profusely. A search for gang members who were responsible for this attack proved fruitless.

To try to stem the senseless violence, I brought together a homosexual gang and a straight gang with the hope that we could intelligently discuss their grievances and thus prevent another conflict. This approach seemed to work initially, so I tried it with several other gangs, but I soon learned that this was an exercise in futility. Whenever it seemed that we might reach a solution, someone would call another gang member a denigrating name. This would set our deliberations back to square one. This happened so frequently that I finally realized that gang members were not bargaining in good faith but were using these meetings as opportunities to be "on stage."

I came to the conclusion that gang problems could best be resolved by those whose expertise was in solving gang problems, and my expertise was in education, certainly not in dealing with gangs. I decided to terminate the meetings with the understanding that gang affiliations would not be recognized in the school. I advised the students that anyone who came to the school to threaten or harm anyone else would be arrested and prosecuted. I made that mandate to all gang members who attended the Benjamin Franklin High School.

While I was struggling to gain a degree of order within the building, a school board member arranged to have a Black Power Conference held at the school on a weekend. Activists from various parts of the United States were brought in for this conference, so I felt that my presence at the school throughout that weekend was necessary. Protecting the school's office equipment and preventing abuse of our telephone service kept me busy. At one point during the conference, my office was commandeered by an activist from California who stationed his bodyguards at the door to prevent me from entering my own office.

During this period in 1968, many of the high schools with large, predominantly black student populations were experiencing militancy by their students. This was especially true at Franklin. The slightest provocation would result in walkouts and demonstrations.

An incident at another high school in South Philadelphia had resulted in acts of violence between the students and the white community, and had been highly publicized by the media. The next day some of the students at Franklin planned a walkout and encouraged other students to join them.

I'd read in the newspaper about the original incident; I knew that school and that principal. When the school board said they would integrate they began by moving the black students from the historically black schools to the white schools. There was anger on both sides, but there was one thing I had already learned: whenever there was change, it was the black students who had to move.

When the students at Franklin decided to protest to demonstrate their loyalty to the students at the other school, it began with some walking out onto Broad Street while others hung out the windows. I knew what had happened at the other school, and I said to myself, "We can handle this. We can do it differently." Broad Street was a commercial area. There were a number of small businesses in the neighborhood; there was a synagogue across the street and a car dealer down the way. There was a junior high school a few blocks away and a girls' high school down the street. All of the people in these stores and schools could have been hurt if things got out of hand at Franklin High School.

Approximately 1,000 students left the school and were milling around at Broad and Green Streets. There was talk of students going two blocks south on Broad Street to the Roman Catholic High School to vent their feelings and show support for students by causing a disruption at that school. I was made aware that the police commissioner had been notified and had sent a busload of officers near the Catholic school to prevent violence.

With the help of some of our teachers and counselors, we were able to get our students back into the school and into the auditorium. They were joined there by some members of the community, most of whom I did not know. There also were others in attendance who had no connection with the community. After hours of discussion, the group strongly urged me to stay through the night to continue the discussion. I informed the superintendent of the situation, and he told me to do what I thought was best. During this all-night discussion, the group made a series of demands that had nothing to do with the walkout. It was now clear to me that the walkout had other purposes.

It did not take very long for the media to become aware of the events taking place, but they were not permitted to enter the school. The students had erected a blockade at the main entrances, and all other doors had been padlocked. I made several excursions through the building to make certain that everything was secure and that the areas where students had gathered were supervised. The auditorium and the gymnasium were being used as sleeping quarters, and all of the upper floors remained dark and uninhabited.

Parents were calling the school for information about their sons, so attendance checks were made and parents were informed about their sons' presence and participation in the all-night demonstration. They were assured that all students were safe and that adequate supervision had been provided by the faculty and staff.

During these hectic hours, members of the community held a separate meeting to discuss how they might become a positive force for good at the school. An Episcopal priest was sent to my office to discuss the role that the community might play in supporting me as principal. I declined the offer because I felt it was most important that I first establish my relationship with the students.

Plans for the next school day were made in order to avoid another episode of chaos. Some teachers were asked to call all the black teachers who were not present during the all-night session and ask them to come to school 1 hour early to provide additional supervision in the auditorium when students who had not participated in the all-night session arrived. The next morning, students reported to their homeroom classes for attendance check, after which I announced over the public address system that school was dismissed for the day.

To insure the safety of the white teachers, I asked them to meet with their department heads in the large music room in the basement. In this setting I explained the events that had transpired during the night. Many of the white teachers were frightened when some of the militant students dressed in dashikis stood at the doorways to the room. Some of these teachers expressed anger at being rejected by their students. They recounted the many things they had done to provide a quality education for the students. There were teachers at the school who had gone above and beyond what was required of them as teachers, and I understood their feelings. However, conditions were becoming volatile, and I feared for the safety of the white teachers.

A black assistant to the superintendent had come to the school, and he quietly gave me some much-needed advice, which caused me to change my plan to send the white teachers home. He was the only person from the school board who came to advise me that day. I was all alone. He made me aware that my sending the teachers home would be a violation of the teachers' contract with the school district.

However, one of the top ranking officers in the police department did convince the teachers to evacuate the school. He informed me that students from two other high schools were on their way down Broad Street to join our students in their demonstration. Some of the teachers heard the conversation and informed the rest of the faculty who then decided on their own volition to leave the school. Three white male teachers refused to leave and joined me in my efforts to secure the building after all non-demonstrating students were sent home.

Early in the morning of the next day, I took a walk outside of the school building with the school community coordinator. This breath of fresh air was just what I needed after a night without sleep. It prepared me for the list of seven demands that I received from the students. The four most important ones that I can recall were:

- assignment of a black coach in a major sport
- inclusion of Swahili as a foreign language in the curriculum
- assignment of a black department head in an academic subject
- change in the name of the school from Benjamin Franklin to Malcolm X High School

The inclusion of Swahili in the curriculum and the securing of a black department head could be achieved with only minimum difficulty. The basketball coach position, however, had been filled for a number of years by a white teacher who was well-liked by the students and the faculty. During his tenure, the basketball team's record was very successful, and in addition, removing him from his position would be a violation of the teachers' contract. As a possible solution, I proposed that the black assistant coach be elevated to the position of co-coach, but the team rejected this proposal and said they would not play unless the black assistant coach was given the position of head coach.

When the white head coach heard of the team's decision not to play for him, he resigned. When he left, the coach had tears in his eyes. He had loved his students and his work, and most of them liked and respected him, but a few militants had gotten to the basketball team, and it became impossible for the white coach to be effective there. I regret to this day that he felt forced to resign. It resolved the immediate problem, but it left me with the realization that I had failed to do all that could be done to avoid the pain that rejection creates.

The one demand that was highly controversial was changing the school's name. Prior to the demonstration, some of the students had gone to the library at the University of Pennsylvania to research the life and works of Benjamin Franklin. During their research, they discovered Franklin's "Achilles heel." The records revealed that Benjamin Franklin, during his early life, was a merchant who bought and sold indentured servants and slaves. Before long, students had reproduced copies of the information they had discovered and distributed them throughout the school's population. They felt that this information would encourage many more of the students to join in this effort and thus would improve their chances of getting the attention of the superintendent and the school board.

The students asked me to inform the superintendent of their rationale for wanting to change the name of the school. I contacted him by telephone and made him aware of the controversy, and the next day, the second day of the demonstration, he told me that the issue would be discussed by a committee of three board members.

I attended this meeting accompanied by several students; however prior to the meeting, I was asked to speak privately with the board committee, and it became clear to me that they did not intend to recommend the name change to the full school board. I advised the committee that meeting with them privately without my students present would undermine my credibility at the school, but they insisted that I join them in this private meeting, and the students immediately expressed concerns that I would be coerced into changing my position on renaming the school.

One board member declared that placing the name of Malcolm X on a school at that time would create chaos. He said that perhaps at some time in the future, Malcolm X might be considered a suitable name for a school in Philadelphia, but not at this time. I returned to the students in the outer office and told them that the full board of education would render a decision in this matter at a later date.

During this period, my efforts to effectuate a positive school climate for learning became increasingly more difficult. Some students felt that I was not "black enough" and that I had sold out to the establishment. To counter that image, I pushed to hold a school referendum on the name change. Prior to this referendum, I had asked the student leaders to tell me what they knew of Benjamin Franklin and Malcolm X.

I discovered that they knew very little about the background of either, so I posed questions for them to answer, "Have you read about the life of Benjamin Franklin? Have you read the autobiography of Malcolm X?" The answer to both questions was "No." I then reminded them that it is unfair to evaluate a man's life by one negative act. You must look at the whole man. I told them that although Franklin had been a broker who bought and sold indentured servants and slaves, he changed and became an abolitionist. I reminded them, too, that Malcolm had been a pimp, a hustler, a womanizer and a thief, but he changed. He embraced the Islamic faith, and espoused inclusion rather than exclusion. He traveled to Mecca where he saw diverse groups of people, white, black, brown and yellow, who had also embraced the Islamic faith and were serving God under the umbrella of Islam. I knew at the time that most of what I said had little impact on the students' points of view, but I hoped that at the very least it would make them think.

The school referendum was held without revealing my position on the name change issue before ballots were cast; however, during the counting of the ballots, I made an announcement on the school's public address system to let the students know that I supported their demand to change the school's name to Malcolm X High School. The referendum overwhelmingly supported the change.

Finally, I was informed, after a whole year had passed, that the Board of Education had denied approval of the name change. To compensate for their disappointment, the students named the school's auditorium "Malcolm X Hall" and the basketball team, the "Malcolm Xers." With these two decisions behind me, I was able to move on and turn my full attention to the educational program.

★ CHAPTER THIRTEEN ★
SPEAKING ABOUT BUCHENWALD

The following school year brought new students who had not been impacted by the militant atmosphere of the previous year's graduating class. This somewhat peaceful interval gave me an opportunity to motivate the newcomers toward more productive endeavors.

As I was giving my best effort to resolve problems at Benjamin Franklin High School in Philadelphia, an incident happened at Bensalem High School in Bucks County, where I lived at the time and still continue to reside.

Male students were told that long hair, mustaches and beards were prohibited in that high school. Some students protested this ruling by holding a sit-in in the school's auditorium and refusing to leave when instructed to do so. Police were called, and the students were forcefully removed from the building and suspended. As a result of these suspensions, parents and friends from the community came together. Some were from Linconia, an all-black community, and others came from the adjoining community, Concord Park, the integrated housing development where I lived. The community members met at a local church to discuss their grievances and ways to support the students. Specifically, they discussed a recent decision by the courts in another venue, which declared that schools had no power to forbid the wearing of long hair, mustaches or beards, and any such ruling by school districts would be deemed unconstitutional.

Armed with this knowledge, the community group decided to march to Bensalem High School the next morning to confront the school administration, but first they needed to choose a spokesman, and I was chosen. I said that I would accept this leadership role on one condition — that it would be a silent, nonviolent march and vigil. Everyone agreed, and with police cars escorting our sizeable group, we headed to the school.

The silence of our integrated group attracted a great deal of attention. Finally, the principal came out, and I made him aware of our purpose. He, in turn, contacted the president of the Bensalem School Board, and after some discussion they finally agreed to meet with members of our group at an appointed time. In the subsequent meeting, the court decision regarding the hair issue was discussed, and the school's ban on long hair and facial hair was declared null and void.

The peaceful, nonviolent action taken by the parents, students and other members of the community had won the day for us but not for the principal. He subsequently decided to leave his position at Bensalem High School, and he accepted an appointment as principal in an out-of-state school district.

GOOD ENOUGH

★ ★ ★

I was in my second year as principal of Franklin High School when the new superintendent of the Philadelphia School District introduced me to a man named George Packard, the new publisher of the now defunct newspaper called *The Evening Bulletin.*

George took me to lunch at the Bellevue Stratford Hotel in Philadelphia. The room was crowded with lunchtime diners, many of whom were politicians whom I recognized. During our conversation over lunch, he asked if I would be interested in running for mayor of Philadelphia. I looked at him, and realized that he was serious. But I was serious too, when I responded with a firm, "No! I am not the person for that job. When you move into the political arena, you are expected to be a team player. They would not have me because I would make my own decisions based on what is right for the citizens of this city." I was quite surprised at the whole incident, but I must admit it was a gratifying experience, and I was flattered to have been considered worthy to hold such a high position.

★ ★ ★

By the mid-1970s the demonstrations and turmoil had calmed, but that didn't mean that there were not still problems at Benjamin Franklin High School. Some of these young men were so damaged, others were so deficient in their education, I didn't know how to deal with teaching these students on a high school level when they didn't even know how to read, or how to teach them to solve their problems through nonviolence when all they had ever seen was violence. There was no one to come to my aid; there was no book to read. The teachers and I were on our own in trying to give these young men an education.

I had just taken on the philosophy of nonviolence and love for everyone that I had heard from Dr. Martin Luther King. One of the ways I decided to help bring this philosophy into the school was by inviting guest speakers from the community to talk to the students. One day I was walking down the hall when I heard a lot of commotion coming from one of the classrooms. The students inside were obviously being very rude, and so I stepped in to see what I could do. The classroom teacher had invited a guest speaker that day; her name was Nina Koleska and she was a survivor of a concentration camp.

"Cool it," I told the students. "Listen to what she is saying because it is important. I was there, and I saw it. You need to hear about it."

I stayed in the room to make sure the students continued to treat her with respect, and I listened to her experiences, and as the students listened it became a wonderful experience for me. I saw them begin to sit quietly and really listen and absorb her pain. Nina had lost her mother, her father, her grandparents and three brothers in the concentration camps. She was the only member of her family to come out alive. The students began to ask her questions.

"When they came for you did you fight back? Did your parents fight back?"

She explained to them how it had been impossible to fight. There were too many soldiers. Those who did fight back were shot and killed on the spot. And there were the children. How could the adults fight back and leave the children unprotected? The price would have been too high. They didn't know where they were going, but they knew if they fought at that time they would be killed right there. Sometimes the price is too high to fight evil in a particular situation; you have to hold on and wait. After she spoke the boys came forward and looked at the numbers on her arm. Then they walked out of that classroom in silence.

She had touched them with her pain. These boys had experienced so much pain in their lives themselves, and they thought that they were the only ones to have ever experienced it. They were angry that they had already missed so much in life. Now they could compare her life with their own. They understood that everyone suffers.

I learned something, too, that day. As I listened to Nina speak I thought to myself, "If she can communicate with these boys and get through to them, what about me? Can I use my experiences to help people learn that there is another way?" I wanted to let my students know where I stood. That I didn't believe that coming out and attacking your problems with a baseball bat was the right way. I wanted to be an agent of nonviolent change. As I listened to Nina I realized that maybe this was the way that I could do that. Nina opened the door for me to begin to speak to others about my experiences in World War II.

I had mentioned being at Buchenwald very briefly to Mary, but I'd never spoken about it much. She didn't know all of it, not the horrors. My parents never knew anything about it. I was never able to bring myself to tell them anything about being there or what I saw. That day at the school, after the students left, I talked with Nina, and she told, "Young man, you have something to say."

Nina wanted me to tell others about my experiences; she talked to some people, and the next thing I knew I was getting calls asking me to be a speaker. One of the early places I spoke was at a meeting sponsored by Temple University. It was held at a hotel in Philadelphia. I didn't know what I should say, but they told me, "It's only fifteen minutes, Leon, you can do that," so I went.

When it was my turn to speak I was surprised at the attention and focus that I received. Most of the people in attendance were Jewish. I was the one black man there. I told them about my experiences as an African American in the military. I talked about how it had felt to be asked to fight and possibly die for a country that wouldn't even let me drink out of the same water fountains as they did. I had been an angry soldier, questioning my own wisdom in joining the Army to fight for freedoms that I wasn't allowed to enjoy. But what I saw at Buchenwald convinced me I had something to fight for, and in the months that followed, as I learned even more about what had happened in Germany, the enormity of it, that twelve million people had died in those camps, six million of them Jews and one and a half million of them children. That's when I knew what I was fighting, for it was the same hate; the hate that bus driver felt in Mississippi when he told me to stand at the back of the bus was the exact same hate, just taken to another level, that had allowed Hitler to kill twelve million people. It was all about saying, "You are not good enough."

★ CHAPTER FOURTEEN ★
LEON, JR. AND DELIA

By the time Leon reached sixth grade, the Vietnam War was raging. I hoped desperately that it would end before he reached that critical draft age, and in 1972, we all were relieved that the Vietnam hostilities had ended, making college a reality for him.

Brown University told him that his grades were adequate for admission, but they had received 10,000 applications with placement for only 1,000 freshmen. It was suggested that Cornell University might be able to accept him. This proved to be the case, and he enrolled at that university.

Prior to Leon's enrollment, there had been a demonstration by black students at Cornell's Student Union. Newspapers across the country carried photographs of militant students brandishing rifles, guns and bandoliers. This was typical of the climate of the times in many of the country's institutions of higher learning.

Leon encountered some of this hostility one day when he went into a lunchroom with some of his white friends. While carrying a tray of food, he saw a table of black students. They called to him, and he went over to meet them. They invited him to take a seat at their table.

"I can't today. I'm eating with some of my friends," he told them.

"Are you with those Honkies?" they asked, pointing to the white friends he had come in with.

"Wait a minute, fellows; you don't know me," my son told them. "No one tells me who my friends are."

When I heard about this incident, my anxiety about his welfare abated somewhat, and I was convinced he could handle himself.

Leon, Jr. graduated from Cornell University in 1976, and we wanted to celebrate with a dinner at an up-scale restaurant. Leon asked if he could bring a friend. Well, "Guess who came to dinner!"

The young lady was short in stature with blond hair and blue eyes. It was a strange feeling to see her standing next to our son who is six feet five inches tall, but we had a wonderful meal and enjoyed the company of a very fine lady.

After his graduation, Leon decided right away that he wanted to move to the west coast. Delia decided that she would like to go along for the ride, and we all thought it was a good idea for Leon to have company on the drive.

It was a hot day in June when Leon and Delia left with the understanding that they would call home every night. Needless to say, we felt insecure when they left our home but we kept a brave face. It took them a full week to reach California. A few weeks later, Mary and I flew to Los Angeles to make sure that Leon was settled in at the home of his Godmother, and to have Delia fly back with us to our home in Bucks County.

GOOD ENOUGH

In a very short time, Leon found a position in a psychiatric hospital working with emotionally disturbed children. He enjoyed this work experience and decided to enroll at the University of California in the School of Social Work. This was a change from his original plan to pursue a law career. I advised him that social workers did not earn very much money, but this did not alter his plans, and he graduated with a Masters Degree in social work.

For more than 6 years, he administered to the needs of emotionally disturbed children. During that time he married and had the responsibility for the care of his two children.

The need for greater income convinced him to enroll in law school at the University of California, Berkeley. He acquired government loans and worked during the summer months to support his family. After a long and difficult time, he graduated from Berkeley Law School.

Leon ,Jr. and Delia with Mary and me

His next hurdle was passing the very difficult California Bar exam, and once he passed that, he was appointed as an assistant in the office of the Los Angeles District Attorney. He became a very successful litigator, but even though he was successful in prosecuting those who broke the law, he was not happy dealing with drug and murder cases.

After leaving the District Attorney's office, Leon joined a firm where he practiced labor law, then took a position as one of several attorneys working for Pacific Con-Edison, an energy corporation, located in Los Angeles. This turned out to be the best move he could have made. He progressed as a litigator and finally advanced to be the top litigator at Pacific Con-Edison, where he remains today.

Leon's two sons are both fine young men. My eldest grandson, Ananda, at age 27, is gainfully employed as a supervisor for the Peet's Tea Company in Los Angeles. Jason, age 24, graduated from San Jose State University and is currently employed as a therapeutic behavioral specialist.

Both Leon, Jr. and Delia attended the George School in Newtown for high school. During her senior year there, Delia was required to complete a project for graduation that rendered a service to a wider community. She chose to go to Liberia, Africa, with a Liberian classmate to teach reading to adults. They were very successful in this endeavor, and Delia gained a wealth of understanding about a different culture.

After graduating from the George School, Delia was accepted at Tufts University in Massachusetts, where she majored in French and City Planning. In 1981, in her senior year at Tufts, two of Delia's white friends were graduating and their apartment in the town of Sommerville,

Massachusetts became available. I was visiting her on the day she went to see the realtor. We went to his office together and approached the counter.

"I've come to rent the apartment that will become vacant when my friends graduate from the University," Delia said to the realtor.

He didn't respond, just went over to his desk and sat down. We waited for him to return to the counter, but he did not come back or acknowledge us. Delia did not seem to be aware of what was happening, but I certainly was. I raised my hand and slapped the counter to get his attention.

He then came over to me, and I advised him that he and I were both aware of the laws against discrimination in rental housing. His face turned red when I said, "We will bring our friends from the NAACP and demonstrate in front of this building."

Of course, I didn't know anyone in the NAACP in Massachusetts, but the realtor didn't know that. He called the building's owner, then came over to us and gathered the necessary papers for us to sign.

When we left that office, Delia said to me, "But, Dad, he doesn't know me." Her statement resonated within me, and I became both angry and sad to think that my daughter had to experience this painful racial rejection. Later in the year, that same realtor came to Delia's apartment and gave her a box of candy.

Delia graduated in 1982 and entered a society that was experiencing a recession. Jobs were at a premium, even for college graduates. My membership on the Penn Charter School Board brought me in contact with the president of Provident Bank in Philadelphia. We spoke often of our children, and I made him aware of my daughter's difficulty in gaining employment. He asked me from which university she had graduated, and when I told him she was a Tufts University graduate, his response was "Send her to my office."

Delia met him at the bank for lunch and was interviewed by four of his department's vice-presidents. This led to 18 months of training and finally a permanent position at Provident Bank.

Banking was at that time, and in many cases continues to be, a predominately white male world fraught with both racism and sexism. Delia had one such experience that brought her home crying. She had left her work on her supervisor's desk for evaluation. When she returned the next day, her supervisor asked for her work. Delia explained what she had done and could not understand why it was not on his desk. Later that morning she found her work in a trash basket. She was very upset that someone had tried to make her appear incompetent and negligent. However, in spite of the racism and sexism, Delia persevered in banking and eventually was promoted to vice-president. She served in that position in private banking with Wachovia Bank for several years before moving on to Wilmington Trust Bank in the same capacity. During this period of professional advancement, Delia also found time to bless our family with two children, Julian Blake Dandridge and Kendall Marie Dandridge, who at the time of this writing are 18 and 10 years of age, respectively. Both are doing well in schools near their home in New Jersey. Julian is now a freshman at Amherst College in Massachusetts.

★ CHAPTER FIFTEEN ★
TIME FOR RETIREMENT

To say that my years at the Benjamin Franklin High School were difficult would be an understatement. The struggle to bring order out of chaos and make the educational process viable took its toll on me. I was drained both physically and psychologically, but I remained at the school for 14 years, and during that time I also pursued and received a doctoral degree in Urban Education at Temple University.

It was in my fourteenth year that I realized I had reached the time to consider retirement. One morning as I was driving to work, my hands began to ache. This continued until I reached school and then stopped while I attended four long meetings. On my drive home the aches returned, and when I arrived at home I described to my wife what was happening and how I felt. She advised me to take a nap, but I could not sleep, so she took me to the hospital. My doctor administered a nitroglycerin tablet, which stopped the aches in my hands, and then proceeded to admit me to the intensive care unit where I was given a series of tests and finally was advised that I had had an attack in the posterior region of my heart.

I remained in the hospital under treatment for approximately 10 days. I was glad to be recovering but sad that I was not permitted to attend the graduation ceremony at Tufts University in Massachusetts where my daughter, Delia, was to receive her Bachelor of Science degree, nor my own graduation ceremony at Temple University where I was to receive my doctoral degree.

I submitted my letter of retirement from the Benjamin Franklin High School in June of 1981.

★ CHAPTER SIXTEEN ★
THE UNITED STATES LIBERATORS CONFERENCE

I had been speaking for several years when, in 1981, I was invited to become a member of a United States delegation to the Liberators Conference being held at the State Department in Washington, DC. Those in attendance came from countries which were allied with the United States during World War II. All of us had been considered liberators of a concentration camp in Europe. The first meeting was a "meet-and-greet" session followed by brief speeches by some of the survivors. Later in the evening we listened to Elie Weisel, a survivor of the Buchenwald Concentration Camp and recipient of the Nobel Peace Prize. His remarks were most eloquent, and he ended by asking all of us, the eyewitnesses and the survivors, to be advocates for peace in the world. I was asked to speak on the following day of my experience as an eyewitness of the evil perpetrated by the Nazis at the Buchenwald

Concentration Camp located just outside the city of Weimar in Germany. In my 15 minutes of sharing, I also spoke of my experiences as a black soldier serving his country in a segregated army.

My remarks were well received, but there was one person, a rabbi, who felt I should not have exposed my country's treatment of its black soldiers.

"We are beyond that stage now," he told me.

"It happened. It was real. Why would I not talk about it?" I responded.

He felt that my remarks had embarrassed my country in front of the Russian delegation. There was a time in my young life when I might not have questioned his comments, but after seeing what the Nazis did at Buchenwald and knowing what I had experienced in Georgia and Mississippi, I knew it was the same hate, and it had to be exposed. If we do not remember our history, we are doomed to repeat it.

My badge from the Liberators Conference

Among the attendees at this conference were members of the media who quickly published my remarks along with my photograph in a B'Nai Brith magazine, which circulated throughout the United States and Canada. At a later date, I received a telephone call from an organization in Vancouver, British Columbia, Canada. The organization invited me to speak at their symposium on the Holocaust, and I agreed to do so.

The caller also told me that there was someone in Vancouver who wanted to speak to me.

I told him that I did not know anyone who lived in Vancouver. The caller then said, "Well, he says he knows you." The stranger got on the telephone and in a very loud and excited voice said, "I know you; you were my messiah! You were my liberator! My name is Robbie Waisman. I saw you when you came into the camp, and I had never seen a black person before. I was 16 years of age, and I was just skin and bone at that time." At the time, I was a young 20-year-old soldier, overwhelmed by what I had experienced at Buchenwald. I had not seen Robbie, but he had seen me, that black face that had amazed him, that face he could not forget. It would be nearly 35 years before he saw me again.

Robbie had relocated and was living in Vancouver, Canada, where there was a group of survivors. They were making plans to hold a Remembrance Day program in memory of the 6,000,000 Jews who had perished in the Holocaust. While reading a B'nai Brith brochure, Robbie had seen my picture accompanied by an article about my speaking at a Liberators Conference

Here I am with Robbie Waisman. We have become good friends over the years and enjoy our meetings.

in Washington, DC. The photograph showed me dressed in my soldier's uniform, and Robbie had recognized me.

My arrival in Vancouver was filled with emotion when I met Robbie and his family at the airport. It was an emotional meeting for both of us, the liberated and the liberator. We hugged and kissed while the Canadian Broadcasting Company televised our meeting.

At the symposium, Robbie was asked to introduce me to the audience. He had never spoken about the loss of his family during the Holocaust, but on this day, as he was introducing me, the tears came down his cheeks, and his pain touched all the listeners.

The Canadian Broadcasting Company followed us and filmed our time together as we traveled around Vancouver. They were with us at the airport as we said our goodbyes, and I left Vancouver for my home near Philadelphia, Pennyslvania.

A few weeks later, I was told that I would be the recipient of the annual humanitarian award given by The Interfaith Council on the Holocaust. Robbie had been asked to come to Philadelphia to make the presentation. The CBC flew with him to Philadelphia and filmed some of the places we visited together. They came to the George School in Bucks County where I was doing some part-time teaching, even though I had retired, and observed me teaching my history class a lesson on the Holocaust.

Several weeks later, Mary telephoned me at school and told me I should come home because I was on television. The CBC had edited all of what they had filmed, with additional footage from the Buchenwald Concentration Camp and submitted it to the McNeal-Lehrer news program for presentation. It was aired on PBS under the title, "A Moment in Time." My telephone began ringing constantly that evening from friends who saw me and said they had never known of my experience. Robbie told me later that the piece had received the award for best short documentary at the Cannes Film festival in 1982.

During the subsequent 25 or so years, we have developed a great friendship. We met in 2008 in Tulsa, Oklahoma, to participate in Yom Ha Shoa, Holocaust Memorial Day, and again a year or so later in New Jersey.

★CHAPTER SEVENTEEN★
NEW EXPERIENCES

"Facing History and Ourselves" is an organization that believes that every school should provide a diverse educational environment for its students and staff. The organization has been on the front lines in the struggle for equality of opportunity, especially in education, and especially at that time, for all the citizens of Boston.

In the early 1980s during the time when attempts were being made to racially desegregate schools in Massachusetts, I was invited to speak at a high school in Boston called Boston English High. Parents and others in the community had been protesting in an effort to prevent racial integration, and police even had to surround the school to protect teachers and students from the protesters. So in this atmosphere and with some apprehension, I arrived at the school, proceeded to the cafeteria where the students were gathered and was met with applause. I was relieved and truly motivated to give my best lecture on the evils of racism, anti-Semitism and the Holocaust, and I shared my life experiences, both good and bad. During the presentation, the audience was so silent you could hear a pin drop. Afterwards, the students asked questions that were provocative and thoughtful.

On this day in Boston, I became a resource person and good friend of the organization, "Facing History and Ourselves." Since then I have traveled with them extensively and have lectured many times on how we must each become a "committee of one" to produce the positive changes that need to be made in our society. This organization has, over the years, afforded me the opportunity to contribute to nonviolent social change and for that I am eternally grateful.

In 1982, I met the new headmaster of the George School, a private Quaker High School, on their tennis courts. Both of my children had attended the George School and had finished college, and I had retired from the Philadelphia School District. When the headmaster learned of my retirement, he asked if I would like to teach in the George School's history department. I was not interested, but after several unsuccessful attempts to recruit me, he offered a compromise. He asked, "Would you be willing to teach 1 hour a day?" This was more in keeping with my retirement schedule, and so I relented and finally agreed.

Students at the George School were assigned to classes homogeneously according to their ability. There were four tracks with the fourth being the highest achieving students. This class created a challenge for me because, as a school administrator, I had not been a classroom teacher for approximately 25 years. The text on American History was written at a college level, so I had to stay at least one chapter ahead of my students, but in just a few weeks, I again felt secure in the classroom. I began to really enjoy what I was doing and was happy that I was no longer in my past role as administrator.

One day while teaching, a student entered the room with a message for me. He said that there was someone on the telephone who needed to speak to me. I told the student to take the message, and I would return the call after class. The student left, only to return saying that a representative of a politician needed to talk to me right away. My students urged me to take the call, which was from a woman representing a nationally-known social and political activist who wanted me to join him on a junket to Bitburg, Germany, but I declined the offer. At this time, there was a controversy about President Ronald Reagan's accepting an invitation to place a wreath on the grave of a German SS soldier, and his acceptance had created a conflict with a large group of his constituency.

A few days later on a Sunday, I was awakened from a deep sleep to answer the telephone. It was again the well-known activist himself calling to extend the invitation again to join him on his trip to Bitburg, but again, I declined the offer. I knew that he was an opportunist and I didn't want to be used.

In the summer of 1986, Mary and I were asked to be a part of a diverse group of Philadelphians on a mission to the Soviet Union to explore the possibility of developing a sister city relationship between Leningrad, now known as St. Petersburg, and Philadelphia. Apparently there was a time when Peter the Great and William Penn had been friends, so the possibility of a renewed relationship, it was hoped, might lead to a citizen exchange program.

This mission to the Soviet Union was the brainchild of a Philadelphia citizens committee organized because of the City Council's failure to respond to the federal government's request for a civil defense plan in the event of a nuclear attack. The committee, instead, opted for a plan of prevention. The committee was comprised of citizens of varied backgrounds, including physicians, teachers, veterans, Philadelphia Orchestra members, politicians and social activists. Some of us, including Mary and me, were members of the Society of Friends. This religious organization, an advocate of peace, played an important role in organizing this visit to the Soviet Union.

Mary and me

The first leg of our journey took us to Helsinki, Finland and then on to Leningrad where we landed safely in spite of rain and fog. As I looked out of the windows, I viewed what I considered an ominous scene, soldiers were carrying machine guns, pistols and other armaments. At customs, we stood in line as our luggage was searched. The customs agent was very abrupt and snatched our passports for examination. Mary and I were the last in line to have our baggage searched, but the customs agent waved us through without any examination. I told Mary that this was the first time that being in the "back of the bus" was an advantage.

We settled into our rather austere room in our hotel on Nevsky Prospect, a main street in Leningrad, and noticed that each floor had a wire gate with a guard to monitor our coming and going. The meals were plain but ample, consisting of potatoes, Brussels sprouts, bread and other staples. Eggs and meat were rarely available. Outside of the hotel, we encountered black market dealers who were eager to purchase anything we had. We could understand why this was so after visiting one of the stores on the main street. The store's inventory was quite sparse, outdated, even shabby and very expensive. On the streets, the pedestrians walked with their heads bowed and appeared depressed.

We observed a line forming outside a small building and thought it probably was a food market, but then realized it was a store that sold vodka. We discovered that the government allowed these vodka stores to remain open for only a few hours each day in order to try to reduce the large number of alcoholics on the streets. Drunkenness on the streets of Leningrad was forbidden, and the law was strictly enforced. We went down into the subway system, the Metro, where at the top of the escalator someone stood guard looking for anyone who might be inclined to vandalize or litter.

Later, our group took a trip on a barge to a museum called The Hermitage. I was surprised to see so many treasures of the czars being maintained in a society that fought a revolution against such opulence. Museums and churches were supported by the government, and many of their fine old buildings were supported and maintained as churches, thus preventing the churches from exacting control over the life of the citizens.

I was very fortunate to become friends with a member of our group who was proficient in the Russian language, and this made it possible for the two of us to meet secretly with some of the local dissenters, "peaceniks" and "refuseniks," as they were called, at the housing project where some of them lived.

One night, my friend and I left our hotel and took a taxicab to the home where we had planned to meet the dissenters. My friend's proficiency with the language enabled us to get to our destination without the taxi driver knowing exactly where we were going. The housing project was very similar to many of the high rise projects in the city of Philadelphia at the time. To protect ourselves and the peaceniks, we left our hotel secretly at 3:00 a.m., although it was not really dark but more like twilight because this was the season of 24-hour nights. We exited our taxi three blocks from our destination so the driver would not know whom we were visiting so early in the morning. We knew that the place we wanted to visit was not part of our tour and visitations were prohibited, so it was important for us to protect those who had invited us to their home.

To get to the apartment of our hosts, we walked up three flights of stairs because the elevator was not working. We entered the small two-room apartment and found approximately 15 people waiting to talk with us. Nearly all of them were graduates of a university with degrees in the mathematics and sciences. Most of them had been incarcerated for violating some law, but the real reason was because they were Jews.

Some had been jailed for their failure to join the Communist Party, and others for trying to obtain a visa to leave the Soviet Union. One young woman, who appeared to be about 20 years old, spoke saying, "I will never have children in a country that persecutes and demeans its citizenry." She also said that she had been placed in an institution where attempts had been made to brainwash her because she disagreed with her government.

I finally understood how difficult their lives were under the Soviet regime, not being allowed to live fully and yet not being allowed to leave. After leaving this meeting, we walked several blocks and hailed a taxicab, which took us back to our hotel without incident where I found Mary still waiting up and upset but relieved that I had returned safely.

During one of our tours around Leningrad, apparently someone in our group violated government instructions on the use of cameras. Certain buildings and other military installations were prohibited from being photographed. The offender was summarily arrested and held by the authorities for 4 hours, then released, but his film was confiscated.

Students from various African countries were attending universities in the Soviet Union, and I had the opportunity talk with one, a native Kenyan. He was not pleased with the way he and the other African students were being treated. The Africans were, of course, required to take a course in Russian language, which then enabled them to understand what was being said about them. He related to me that the remarks were often offensive, racist and denigrating. According to this student, the university's academic offerings and standards were excellent, but they (the Africans) were not considered to be worthy. They were not good enough.

There were also problems when the students wanted to visit their homes in Africa. The Soviet Union initially denied them any travel arrangements that would take them through England because of England's capitalist economy. The students protested, and the Soviet government finally acquiesced to the students' travel demands. During my encounter with the Kenyan student, I was convinced when he said to me, "I am here for one thing and that is to get my education, and as soon as I have achieved that, I am going home to Kenya."

On our last day in Leningrad, we attended a circus, and that same evening we were entertained by a Russian dance group, which included the Cossack dancers with their amazing athleticism, stamina and dexterity. Unfortunately, our trip was not as successful as we had hoped. We had been unable to meet with those in leadership positions in education, the arts and the government, who for various reasons were not available to meet with us. The return trip to the United States was uneventful, just what I wanted, but the memories of this large, diverse, complicated country will last forever.

★ ★ ★

The organization, Facing History and Ourselves, Inc., which I referred to previously, sponsored a civil rights study tour to begin May 2, 2001. Because of previous commitments, I joined the tour late in Detroit. There I met and made many friends from cities across our country. We traveled from Detroit, Michigan, to Montgomery, Alabama, and arrived in Birmingham on the day that a Ku Klux Klansman, Thomas E. Blanton, Jr., was convicted of the murder of four black girls in the 1963 bombing of the Street Baptist Church. That night a vigil was held at the church in remembrance of the four young girls who had lost their lives in the struggle for freedom. Along with some of my friends, I walked from our hotel to the vigil area. As we walked, I engaged in a conversation with a French woman, Pascale. We spoke of the martyrs whose names we were both familiar with as well as the unknown foot soldiers who should also be recognized and honored.

We stood at the church facing the steps leading to the entrance and saw seated at the top of the steps near the entrance the mother of one of the slain girls and the father of another. After the singing of some freedom songs, we listened intently as each parent spoke briefly, sharing their pain with all who were assembled. I was particularly moved by the father of Denise McNair, one of the victims of the bombing, as he spoke of the tragic loss of his daughter. This was followed by a brief candle-lighting ceremony.

The next day we returned to the church and met in small groups with a facilitator assigned to each. The discussions were lively and stimulating, and the passion of the leader became my passion. The question we were asked to answer as a group and as individuals was "When did you become aware of and affiliated with the Civil Rights Movement?" The question puzzled me because I could not remember any single event that made me suddenly cognizant of the need for nonviolent social change, but certainly there was the cumulative effect of years of slights and insults of racism.

Many of the events that led to my awareness and participation in the struggle for equality began when I volunteered to be a soldier in the United States Army. The evils of racism experienced in living and training as a soldier in the Deep South had surely scarred my psyche, and it was a daily struggle to hold my anger in check and keep it from turning into hatred. But the values instilled in me by my parents kept me on the right path, and one day the clarion voice of Dr. Martin Luther King, Jr. touched me in a way unlike any way I had ever been touched before. I marveled at his "I Have a Dream" speech and absorbed his constant reminder that the changes we all sought had to be made through nonviolent means. His life and his struggle created in me the strong desire to become an agent of change. I know now that it was Dr. King's philosophy that led me to "Facing History" and to Birmingham, Alabama.

Later that day, I was privileged to listen to the Reverend Fred L. Shuttlesworth who shared with us the history of the struggle to end segregation in Birmingham. The next stop on our tour was Montgomery, Alabama, where we visited the Civil Rights Memorial designed by the architect Maya Lin. This was an emotional and moving experience for me as I read the names of some of the heroes in the Civil Rights Movement. At the Poverty Law Center, six young attorneys shared with us details of some of the more interesting cases they had litigated. In one instance the Poverty Law Center attorneys sued the Ku Klux Klan for commission of a hate crime and won 6.2 million dollars for their clients. In addition, the compound belonging to the

Aryan Nation, a related neo-Nazi group, valued at $250,000, was seized as part of the penalty for the burning of a church in Macedonia, Alabama. It was interesting to discover that at that time the Aryan Nation was being financed heavily by millionaires living in the Silicon Valley of California.

On the day our tour group arrived in Selma, Alabama, we were met by some of the "foot soldiers" who told of how they were viciously attacked during a peaceful march on what is now known as "Bloody Sunday," March 7, 1965, when some 600 civil rights marchers were met on the Edmund Pettus Bridge where state and local lawmen attacked them with tear gas and billy clubs. Prior to that event, we were told, Sheriff Jim Clark had entered a black church in Selma and pulled the preacher from the pulpit, handcuffed him and dragged him down the aisle and out the door. This act of brutality was one of many attempts to instill fear in the hearts of its black citizens.

Next on our tour was Jackson, Mississippi, where we arrived on May 6, 2001. A meeting had been arranged with some of the Jewish community who were seated on a stage as we arrived. A rabbi with a small congregation talked to us of the climate of fear in Jackson and other cities in Mississippi.

He spoke of one man who was told by the White Citizens Council that he must fire one of his black employees. The employer refused saying, "He has been with me for many years and is one of my best workers." As a result of his refusal, he was unable to get goods and services for his business; his loan at the bank was called; white customers boycotted his store, and he ultimately had to close his business.

Just seven miles north of Jackson sits Tougaloo College, a historically black 4-year liberal arts college, and our stop there brought back memories of my days as a young soldier stationed at Camp McCain near Grenada,

Mississippi. As previously mentioned, my unit, the 183rd Engineering Combat Battalion, trained there, and I had many pleasant experiences during my stay at Camp McCain and my visits to Tougaloo College. Whenever I entered the gates of that institution, I felt as if I was no longer in Mississippi. It had a diverse teaching staff, racially and geographically. I learned many years later that some of the staff were Jewish refugees who had left Europe to escape anti-Semitism and the Holocaust. Some of the white universities refused them employment, so they found employment at the black colleges. I savored the memories of the brief escape I had almost every weekend from racism and the haven I found at Tougaloo.

Jackson, Mississippi, was also the home of Medgar Evers, one of the great civil rights leaders and field secretary for the NAACP, who was martyred for his efforts to make freedom a reality for all. I entered the home of this courageous man, and walked on the driveway where he had been shot and killed on June 12, 1963. It took three trials over 3 decades before Byron de la Beckwith was finally convicted and served life in prison for the assassination of Medgar Evers.

On my last day of the Civil Rights Study Tour, I was privileged to listen to a speech by a brave civil rights champion and former Chairman of the Student Nonviolent Coordinating Committee (SNCC), Congressman John Lewis. I recognized him as one of the faces I had seen many years ago on television being attacked during that infamous "Bloody Sunday" I referred to earlier. He had been considered one of the primary leaders of the Civil Rights Movement, a keynote speaker at the 1963 March on Washington and a Mississippi voter registration coordinator.

This hero subsequently became a member of the United States Congress where he continues to serve, representing Georgia's fifth district and standing strong on issues that touch the lives of all Americans. He personifies the nonviolent philosophy of Dr. Martin Luther King, Jr. and has never deviated from that position.

In 1997 Mary and I had an opportunity to visit South Africa. We learned of the trip through a good friend and member of Salem Baptist Church in Jenkintown, the sponsor of the tour.

We arrived in Johannesburg, South Africa, after a 14-hour flight and immediately boarded another plane to Cape Town where our tour began. During a walking tour, we had the opportunity to meet and talk with uniformed school children and their teachers.

At the time of our visit, apartheid legally had ended, but the divisions were still obvious, the population was still identified as "white," "colored" or "black," schools were still segregated and the black schools, according to our sources, still were not receiving an equal share of educational funding. In spite of these concerns, many people felt that progress was being made under the presidency of Nelson Mandela.

On our way to visit some of South Africa's vineyards, we passed through the "shantytowns" that surround Cape Town. The structures, made of any materials that could be salvaged and huddled together for miles, were deplorable, and the impact was distressing. Sanitation was almost nonexistent and very little medical service was available.

Returning from Cape Town, we had the opportunity to visit the Victor Verster Prison, the prison where Mandela spent the last 4 months of his imprisonment and from which he was finally released, and we stood in front of the gate where journalists and photographers had recorded his walk to freedom on February 11, 1990.

Another highlight of our South African tour was the Ksuger Animal Reserve where we spent 4 days. Every morning from 6 to 9 a.m. we would go out on a game drive, return to our lodge for breakfast, then venture out for another game drive from 4 to 7 p.m. While on safari, we rode in open Land Rovers driven by a park ranger with a tracker, sitting on a high seat in the front of the vehicle. They were amazing in their ability to track the animals through the bush, and we were able to get "up close and personal" within a few feet of many, many animal species including lions, elephants, a leopard, buffaloes, a white rhinoceros, all referred to as the "big five" and considered to be the most dangerous animals in South Africa. On one occasion, I was permitted to approach a rhinoceros, a most unpredictable animal, with great care behind an armed ranger. When the ranger stopped, I stopped. When he said, "Back up," I did so. Then we got back into the Land Rover. Some of the animals came close to look us over, while others seemed to ignore us. Unlike in zoos, this was their natural habitat, they were in charge, they tolerated us and we gave them respect.

Despite the poverty, despite the inequality that still exists, it is a beautiful and complex country, and there is evidence that slowly progress is being made.

GOOD ENOUGH

★ CHAPTER EIGHTEEN ★
PENNSWOOD VILLAGE

After our return from South Africa, Mary began to show signs of what our doctor called "short-term memory loss." The effects of this condition included episodes such as getting lost while driving, misplacing keys, purse and other items, neglecting personal grooming and sometimes requiring assistance while walking. We were fortunate to have placed a deposit previously to be wait-listed at a continuing care retirement community called Pennswood Village, which was capable of providing independent living, assisted living and nursing care. In only a few months, Pennswood called to advise us that an independent residence was available.

The next important task was to sell our home and to sell or dispose of our furniture and other articles that we had accumulated over many years. On January 4, 1998, Mary and I moved into our apartment in Pennswood

Village where we spent several wonderful years together enjoying all they had to offer. During that period, I was able to provide all the care that Mary needed; however, as her Alzheimer's disease progressed, I was no longer able to fully care for Mary alone. The staff doctors recommended transferring Mary from our apartment to the health center, a smaller section within Pennswood called Preston. There she received daily tender loving care by wonderful caring nurses and nursing assistants. I was able to visit and be with her each day until she succumbed to the disease while sleeping peacefully on November 11, 2001.

I continue living in the same apartment with all the good memories of our 53 years of marriage. My life has been dedicated to being an agent of nonviolent social change, and I remain active and travel extensively throughout the United States speaking at universities, churches, high schools and synagogues. I continue my association as a resource person with Facing History and Ourselves, Inc. and a consortium of similar organizations committed to peace and the elimination of racism, sexism and anti-Semitism.

★ CHAPTER NINETEEN ★
GOOD ENOUGH

My memories have been a long way in which I could explain how many of the events of the Twentieth Century made an impact on my life. It was my mother and father who constantly reminded me in my early years that I was good enough to do and to be anything I wanted to be. They instilled in me the values of kindness, compassion and a respect for others no matter who or what they were. I didn't know when I was growing up that my parents were instilling in me what I needed; they had come through it, and they knew what I would need. They knew I would have to be better than those who would tell me I was not good enough.

In school I saw black teachers who had made it. They knew they were good enough, and they passed that knowledge on to me. To this day I'm appreciative that they saw in me something I did not even see in myself at that time.

Growing up, there were also many people who were telling me in so many ways that I wasn't good enough. The military put a lot of things in the way. "You can't be a sergeant; you can't go to officer's training. You are not as good as those white fellows." The damage was done to so many, both white and black, because if you hear it often enough, you start to believe it.

My parents had given me a shield so that I could battle against the pressure. I didn't think I had all the things I needed. I hadn't always paid attention or learned all I could in school, but what I had gotten from both my parents and my teachers was the understanding that you have to learn to love other people, even though they don't love you. That is the most difficult lesson I ever learned.

One of the most horrendous events in my life was the day that I went into the camp called Buchenwald. I was just 20 years old, and I was totally unprepared for what I saw when I walked through those gates. It has impacted me for the rest of my life, I will never forget it. The horror and the suffering of people who had been denied anything that would make life livable was beyond belief. There was very little I could do about the suffering at the time. I was not a doctor, I was merely an eyewitness. But the mere fact that I saw the results of bigotry and hatred made me know that if I got out of the war alive I would try to effect change in the lives of others who were suffering.

The day that I heard Dr. Martin Luther King's "I Have a Dream" speech in Washington, D.C., was a day I will never forget. Listening to that speech made me know that I was good enough to become an agent of nonviolent social change. I was part of 250,000 people all trying to create a change. At the Lincoln Memorial I could see all the way up to the microphones. I stood there watching as Dr. King began to speak. His words, the sound of his voice captured me.

He talked about his dream, about little children playing together, and tears came down my face. I knew I was in the presence of greatness, of a true leader. His example was part of my motivation. He had an impact on my life that I will never forget. His spirit, his willingness not only to work so hard, but to die for what he believed made me want to live up to the standards that he had set, to keep believing in myself, that I was good enough; to not be afraid of the price I might have to pay to do the right thing. That is what I carry with me day. As a teacher, that is what I tried to tell the children, that it is not easy.

Today, I'm able to think about my life, about how things have changed and the things that are happening today. We still have concerns today; the struggle is not over, the hate is still with us. It is a little more subtle today. They don't come at you with a white sheet or a gun, but there are little things that people do. There are places you shouldn't go and things you shouldn't do, but with every step you take in the right direction, you get stronger.

When you are confronted by something that is wrong, ask yourself, "Is the price too high?" Make an assessment of what confronts you. Be wise enough not to put yourself in harm's way, try to keep your family from being hurt. But if you back away from doing the right thing when the price is not too high, you are taking a step backward; you are not living up to the dream. We don't always know what is the right choice; we can only hope to do what is best. There are no guarantees, we can only try. Just be prepared to make a decision, and only hope to make the right one.

I met Attorney General Eric Holder at the Holocaust Remembrance Days observance in April 2010. The inscription on the lower photo reads: "With thanks for the better world you created. Eric Holder"

★ ABOUT THE AUTHOR ★

Dr. Leon Bass is a former high school principal and veteran of World War II who has dedicated much of his life as a teacher, a school administrator and a speaker, to fighting racism wherever it exists.

Following his service in the U.S. Army 183rd Engineer Combat Battalion in World War II, Dr. Bass graduated from West Chester University of Pennsylvania and later received a doctorate from Temple University. He taught at several schools in the School District of Philadelphia and was a principal at the Benjamin Franklin High School in Philadelphia for 14 years.

He has presented his story to audiences throughout the United States and the world. He was a participant in the International Liberators Conference, held in Washington, DC in 1981. In 1994 he was the keynote speaker at the Georgia Commission on the Holocaust, and in 1996 he was awarded the Pearlman Award for Humanitarian Advancement from Jewish Women International. He appeared in the Academy Award-nominated documentary "Liberators: Fighting on Two Fronts in World War II." You can learn more about Dr. Bass at www.DrLeonBass.com.

CPSIA information can be obtained at www.ICGtesting.com
Printed in the USA
LVOW090003210212

269593LV00001B/4/P